EMPATH

Psychic Empathy: Restore Your Health, Control
Your Emotion Skills and Protect Yourself From
Narcissistic Abuse

(Manage Your Empathy and Develop Your
Spiritual Gift)

Debbie Elisabeth

Published by Kevin Dennis

Debbie Elisabeth

Empath: Psychic Empathy: Restore Your Health, Control Your Emotion Skills and Protect Yourself From Narcissistic Abuse (Manage Your Empathy and Develop Your Spiritual Gift)

ISBN 978-1-989920-49-7

Legal & Disclaimer

The information contained in this book is not designed to replace or take the place of any form of medicine or professional medical advice. The information in this book has been provided for educational and entertainment purposes only.

The information contained in this book has been compiled from sources deemed reliable, and it is accurate to the best of the Author's knowledge; however, the Author cannot guarantee its accuracy and validity and cannot be held liable for any errors or omissions. Changes are periodically made to this book. You must consult your doctor or get professional medical advice before using any of the

Table of Contents

Chapter 1: What Is Empathy

Empathy is being aware of the emotions and feelings being experienced by other people, and understanding them as if you are experiencing them too. Being empathetic is a key aspect of developing your emotional intelligence, for you get to form a connection between yourself and other people and their feelings. Empathy, unlike sympathy, which is just feeling pity for what a person might be going through, goes further to feel together with a person. Basically, empathy is the capacity to comprehend the emotions of another person and may transcend to a deeper level of emotional reaction fueled by the feelings you observe in another person. While to some people, empathy is a skill that comes naturally, it is also a skill that you can develop over time.

Ability to Comprehend Other People

Empathetic people have the ability to sense the feelings coursing in another person and getting concerned about their emotions. To fully comprehend another person, you have to pay great attention to what another person is not letting you see through their speech. Look at their nonverbal cues and the hints that they drop, albeit in a subtle manner. You will have to be a great listener, understanding the meaning behind their words that might be veiled, also looking at their body language. When you've observed their emotions, be sensitive towards them, viewing the pain they are going through from their standpoint. You can, from that point, then offer a helping hand to mitigate the problems they might be facing.

Building up Others

This aspect of being empathetic involves giving positive feedback to people for their accomplishments and praising them for the work done. Being empathetic to build and develop others is a leadership trait that you would require to have in honing your leadership skills. Building and developing others also include mentoring them to attain and achieve their fullest potential and encouraging them to achieve the highest standards. Delegate work to people if you are in a leadership position to grow and develop their skills.

Be Service-Oriented
In a work environment, being service-oriented means that you are keen to place the needs of the customers at a top priority. You maintain loyal customers all through, for you seek to always meet their needs first. A relationship of trust is, therefore, maintained between you as an employer and your customers. To meet their needs, tailor your services in such a way that satisfies them.

Types of Empathy
There are three types that are classified as: emotional, compassionate, and

cognitive. On cognitive empathy, it is the use of observation and analytical skills to understand the emotions in a person. Cognitive empathy is more on the rational side of comprehending emotions. Emotional empathy is feeling another person's emotions as your own, and experiencing them as your own. On compassionate empathy, you not only get to comprehend and feel what another person is going through but also take steps to help them. You solve their problems to lighten their pain.

Chapter 2: What Type Of Empath Are You?

There are various kinds of empaths on the planet today. An empath's ability to feel depends largely on how mindful they are. Each empath is unique, and generally has a wide range of qualities in varying degrees.

You can tell one kind of empath apart from another by what characteristics are more dominant in them.Before we jump right into the different types of empaths, here's a caveat: You might find that you fit into more than one category. That's because this is not necessarily a fixed, precise science.

Just like no one is completely melancholic, choleric, phlegmatic, or sanguine, it's rare to find empaths who are exactly just one kind. To avoid any unnecessary confusion, you alone can tell which type of empath you are most like, and which type also describes you, but to a more insignificant degree.

TYPES OF EMPATHS
The Emotional Empath

The emotional empath usually senses other people's emotions. As she has mastered her gift, she can choose not to absorb these emotions. He feels these emotions as if they were his own. She is able to easily tell when someone else is feeling depressed, sad, excited, or joyful.

As an emotionally receptive empath, you never have to ask before you know what's eating someone. You already can tell just how they're feeling, even if you can't tell why they feel that way at the time. You're a natural at connecting with people on an emotional level. Because of this, you're quite relatable. It's also tremendously difficult for people to hide their true feelings from you, or tell you a lie and get away with it.

As an emotional empath, you're highly sensitive. The challenges with you battle everyday on account of how sensitive you are, are beyond imaginable. You're a sponge, soaking up every emotion there is around you. This feels like an invasion, and can be quite confusing, as you feel a wide range of emotions - positive and negative, all at the same time.

All the joy, sadness, malevolence, and benevolence around you can pull you in many different directions at once - especially if you haven't yet learned to keep yourself centered or grounded in the face of that emotional storm. This makes it hard for you to set up established boundaries, and even harder for you to tell where your emotions end and where another's begin.

See, it's very easy to get distracted by this ability to draw from the energy around you. Sometimes it feels like you are a vessel just used to carry what other people feel. It is at this point that emotional empathy becomes very unhealthy. Instead of being something that gives you purpose, it becomes something that sucks the living daylights out of you.

The Spiritual Empath

Spiritual empaths are able to create direct connections to other realms. They are also known as medium empaths. They are able to create connections between the living and deceased and some other spiritual entities in their belief system.

"Spirituality is discovering and connecting with your True Self at the core of your being, and seeing how you connect with all that is."
-Mama Indigo

The Indigo Child's Survival Guide

With their psychic empathic abilities, they are able to feel emotional and physical responses from their communication with the spiritual world. This is works very much in the same way as with the emotional empath, who absorbs energy and emotions from his or her immediate surroundings.

The spiritual empath has the rare ability to sense the emotions of those who have passed on. They can even sense what it was like for them to pass on from this world, to the world beyond.

The Physical Empath

Physical empaths are able to feel where a person's pains and illnesses are when they are around that person. As a physical empath, you can tell exactly what symptoms someone else has. You can even pinpoint the exact location of the pain in their body, without being told.

This might sound a bit nuts, but if you're a physical empath, you can actually feel the same pain in your body! If someone else is feeling weak, it doesn't matter if you had ten hours of sleep and three cups of coffee. You're going to feel just as weak too!

The Intuitive Empath

As an intuitive empath, you have a finely honed sense of knowing. It's a certainty that you feel on a gut level. You're able to tell when someone's lying through their teeth to you, even if they're delivering an Oscar award winning performance. You can tell what people's true intentions really are, without any physical or obvious proof. You can just sense when someone "isn't quite right.

Do you usually have dreams that come to pass? Then you are definitely an intuitive empath. You have the rare and special gift of precognition!

Sometimes, your precognition takes the form of déjà vu, where it seems like you've already seen or experienced something before. At some point, you may have felt a sense of foreboding. You know, the feeling you get where the hairs at the back of your neck stand up straight.

Intellectual Empath

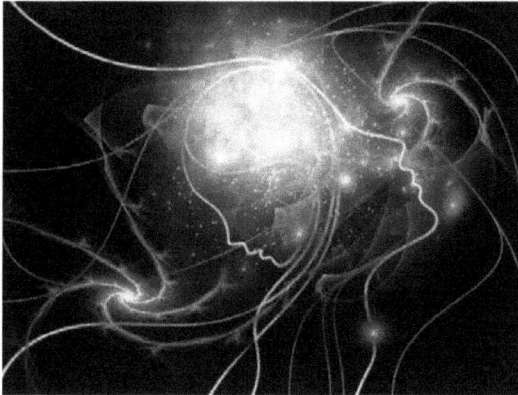

As an intellectual empath, you have above average intelligence. You have a rare, exceptional ability to communicate with all sorts of people, in many ways. You're able to adjust your style of communication, so that whoever you're speaking with in the moment can understand what you're saying perfectly.

What this means is you've got quite a great grasp of language, and you have the perfect vocabulary for the occasion. Not only that, even your mannerisms tend to match those of the people you're addressing. It's not like you're being a phony, or you're deliberately mirroring them. It just comes naturally to you, and on account of this, people are able to feel at home with you. Cool right?

More often than not, you already know what someone wants to say before they even get a word out. No, you're not like those overly obnoxious people who finish other people's sentences and are way off the mark. You know exactly where someone's headed with what they're saying, way before they get there! So when you are completing sentences, you're usually spot on.

The Animal Empath

You can tell you're an animal empath by your uncanny ability to communicate with animals. You're the one your friends and family call "the insert-random-animal-here whisperer." You're very able to sense what animals around you are feeling, or what they need.

You connect with these animals on a level that is beyond deep. You love them fiercely, and you feel everything that they feel. If you're an animal empath, chances are that you actually prefer to be in the company of animals, than with other humans! The animals love you, too. They're unable to resist the pull they feel to you. You're usually the one person who can safely pet that fierce, badly behaved dog without getting your hand chomped off.

How many times have you found yourself relating that huge problem at work to that cute little dog or cat you have at home, and they actually seem to understand you? Ever consider that they may actually understand you? How cool is that?

The Environmental Empath

If you're an environmental empath, you can sense any physical change or disruption in the environment. You can sense tell if there's been some trouble or disturbance in the room before you walked in. In fact, you can sense trouble way before it even happens! You can also tell when it's time to leave, and when you should head somewhere in particular, because you might be needed there, or you might have a meaningful encounter with a situation or a person.

Environmental empaths are also psychometric empaths. If you're one of these, then you have the ability to "read" objects. When you enter a room or a new environment, you can get information about what happened there, or about the people there. All you have to do is simply touch or hold an object in the room, and with that alone, you're able to pick up on information no one else can.

The Plant Empath

As a plant empath, you may have been referred to as a "green thumb," because of how great you are at nurturing plants and helping them flourish. You have a very strong connection to all plants, and trees. You can tell what each plant needs, and you can also sense what each one offers.

As a plant empath, you do very well in nature. You have amazing gardening skills. There could never ever be a dying plant wherever you are. Plants do mighty fine in your presence!

The Heyoka Empath

"Heyoka" is a native American term meaning "sacred clown," or the "fool." No, before you decide this definitely isn't you,

18

being a Heyoka empath is actually a good thing. As a Heyoka empath, the way you connect with people and heal them, is with humor. No joke!

As a Heyoka, what you do is cause a disruption to the usual way of things, so you can help the people around you to gain more clarity on whatever it is they're facing. This disruption is definitely positive, not negative. You have the ability to move yourself between the spiritual and physical realms, and to act as a medium between both worlds. You soak up other people's emotions and feelings, acting as a reflective surface, showing others what they need to see about themselves, whether good or bad.

So there you have it! Very simple, straightforward descriptions of the different types of empaths there are. Like I said before, it is very possible to possess one or more, or even all these traits. A good rule of thumb to figuring out exactly what kind of empath you are, is to focus on the traits that predominantly describe you.

Now I've given you the lowdown on who an empath is. By now you must have figured out what kind of empath you are. So I have a question for you. How do you feel about it all? Good? Bad? Indifferent? Do you feel blessed, or cursed? Should you be thankful? Let's see in the next chapter.

Chapter 3: Who Is An Empath - Are You One? Knowing How To Tell

After having defined empathy, you might be wondering if you really fit the mold of an empathetic person. First of all, we all have the capability of being empathic. While some folks have a more naturally tuned sense of empathy, others may need to work on it a bit more in order to better develop this trait. Nevertheless, you have everything you need to become truly empathetic.

Perhaps the best way for you to get started tuning your empathetic skills is to consistently think about how others feel in any given situation. This is a mental exercise in which you can take any situation, both good and bad, and really try to place yourself is that person's shoes. In order to make the exercise work, you must transport yourself to the situation in which that person finds themselves in. Then, you need to think about what you would or how you would do things if you were in that situation. From there, you can begin to gain a deeper insight into what that person is going through.

Let's consider this example:
A person you know has lost their beloved pet.
Now, if you have lost a pet before, it wouldn't be too hard for you to relate to this experience. In fact, hearing about this

person's loss may take you back to when you lost your own pet. This may end up triggering feelings of sadness and grief as you recollect on what that experience was like for you. You may offer solace to this person by listening to their feelings and sharing your own experience. Often times, people simply need to hear that they are not crazy for feeling the way they do. Moreover, people take great comfort in knowing that what they are feeling is perfectly normal. The last thing anyone wants to feel when going through the painful experience is to feel like an outlier.

On the flipside, suppose that you have never lost a pet in your life. What's more, you have never even owned a pet. So, you really don't have a frame of reference from which you can derive meaning to comprehend what this person is going through.

Nevertheless, you try to become truly empathetic. So, you take yourself to the place where you owned a pet and subsequently lost it. Perhaps you might be able to identify with the loss of a pet *per se*, but you are certainly capable of identifying with the feeling of loss. Perhaps you have lost a family member or have experienced other types of loss such as destruction of property resulting from a natural disaster.

When you begin to place yourself in the same place where the other person is coming from, your own experiences begin to serve as a frame reference. So, you might think, "I don't know what it's like to lose my beloved dog, but I do know what it's like to lose your home in a flood". That is where empathy begins to take hold of you. This exercise may even trigger feelings that you "gotten over".

As you begin to further develop your feelings of empathy, you will notice how you will become more susceptible to the suffering of others. By the same token, you will also begin to relish in the success and happiness of others.

For instance, one of your best friends is getting married to their sweetheart. If you are single and never been married, it might be a bit hard to place yourself in the middle of a wedding, but seeing the happiness and joy of the newlyweds, you being to think, "what is a truly happy moment in my life?" When you think about when you felt over the moon, then you can empathize with your friends and think, "if they feel anywhere close to the way I felt then, they are truly lucky to have each other".

In contrast, a selfish person would resent the married couple because the spotlight is not on them. Do you see where the difference lies?

Consequently, we are going to delve further into specific signs that will alert you that you are an empathic person and not just paying lip service to others who are going through a rough time.

You make others' emotions your own
Before we get into this, a disclaimer: this first point is not about taking on someone else's burden as your own nor should you

attempt to take credit for someone else's success (even if you played a pivotal role in their achievement).

What this first point highlight is the fact that you are willing to internalize others' feelings in such a way that you place yourself directly in their situation. You are keen on understanding what they are going through, both good and bad, as opposed to superficially commenting on what it must be like.

In addition, you are willing to offer emotional support if you are asked to do so. Unsolicited support or advice may rub some folks the wrong way especially if they are too proud to seek help or advice.

So, if you are willing to take the feelings of others to heart, then you are well on your way to becoming a truly empathetic person.

You experience sudden and overwhelming emotions
As an empath, you might find yourself suddenly becoming overwhelmed by

emotions. These instances can happen at any time especially in the middle of a highly emotional situation. For example, you are listening to a testimonial from someone who has gone through a challenging situation. Or, you are listening to someone's story about how they overcame adversity.

Regardless of the specific situation, you find that you are very much in tune with the feelings of others who are attempting to convey. While it is certainly a lot easier to experience these sudden flashes of emotion in a personal, one on one setting, it is highly probable that might become overwhelmed by emotion in a public setting.

For example, you are attending a church service. During the service, you listen to the story of fellow churchgoers who have overcome difficulties in life. The stories you hear are filled with so much emotion that it is impossible for you to contain your own emotions. As a result, you might begin to shed tears or overcome with joy.

In other situations, you might be talking with a friend. This friend might have important news to share with you. When you hear about how good things are going for them, you automatically become overwhelmed by sheer joy and happiness. You are really putting yourself in your friend's spot. So, you might not have anything to say to them other than simply basking in their success.

As you get more and more attuned to your inner feelings, you will find that it is not hard to connect to other folks on a deeper, emotional level. All you have to do is listen to their own feelings and then pay attention to yours. So, don't fight back, just go with the flow.

You get where people are coming from

This is a knack people develop over time due to their own life experience. As you get older and go through various experiences, you begin to appreciate where people are coming from, that is, what causes them to feel and act the way they do.

As such, you are able to connect with people because you understand the underlying factors that are motivating them to do what they do and feel the way they feel. In a way, you do not simply feel what they feel, but you can actually relate to the reasoning behind their actions and emotions.

Consider this example:

A friend has lost their job. They are devastated by the situation and decide they need a change of scenery. So, they take a job overseas that don't necessarily pay well but offers a fresh start.

As an empath, you understand how distraught your friend feels at the loss of their job. At the same time, you understand why they need a change of scenery. In fact, you totally get it to a point where you would have done the same if you had been in the same spot. So, rather than judging your friend for "bailing out" you praise them for making a tough choice and moving on with their life.

Thus, you have connected with your friend at a deeper level. Since you really get where they are coming from, you end up being supportive of their decision. You might even offer your help in any way you can. Now, you might personally feel apprehensive about the decision your friend has taken, but you trust that it's in their best interest.

Others seek you out

Empaths characterize themselves for their lack of judgment. While they may disagree with the actions and decisions that others may choose to make, they don't openly judge anyone. In fact, empaths may even take someone else's side even though they disagree with their decisions.

As a result, others seek your advice and wisdom. Often, they seek you because they know you're a good listener and won't judge them unfairly. This is so important when folks are going through usual circumstances or take unconventional roads.

Moreover, when others seek your advice, they know that you really mean what you say. The words you utter are not superficially commented on shallow observations. You are sincere in your words and would not purposely say something hurtful just for the sake of it. As a matter of fact, if you call someone out on something, it is because you really have the moral high ground to do so. Yet, an empath would do so unless they felt it was beneficial to the other person.

When you are recognized as a true empath (though people may not consciously know it), you will find people opening up to you in ways you would have never imagined possible. But please bear in mind that many times all you need to do is listen without jumping to any conclusions. Often, all most people want is someone who will let them speak their minds.

You are too sensitive to violence in film and television

Gratuitous violence on television and in the film has desensitized people in unimaginable ways. Children and teenagers are exposed to violence from a very young age. And while it is beneficial to become aware of the tragedies in life to a certain extent, empaths struggle with graphic scenes on television and in film. Of course, scenes in movies and TV shows are not actually real, they do depict situations which trigger feelings of pain and suffering for the people going through those acts. This is especially true if an empath has been through a similar situation. For instance, if you, as an empath, have been in a car accident, scenes of car wracks may trigger feelings of fear and pain stemming from your own experience. Consequently, you may choose to avoid watching such scenes altogether.

So, if you feel easily offended and overwhelmed by graphic scenes in television and in film, you need not feel ashamed or embarrassed; quite the opposite, you should feel proud of being sensitive to the suffering of others.

You have a soft spot for kids and animals
If you find that you have a soft spot for kids and animals, then chances are you are far more sensitive than you think. Empaths are usually drawn to babies and cute furry pets. But feelings of empathy don't just apply to cuteness.

True empaths love all kids and animals. They are concerned with the feelings of children in all circumstances while also being very attentive to the needs of animals. An empath would never stand for cruelty to animals. In fact, empaths are the first to offer their help and support in the protection of animals.

Similarly, empaths are always kind to children. They understand that kids are vulnerable and have very sensitive feelings. So, the last thing they want is to hurt a child's feelings. In fact, they will be the first to offer comfort to a child who is upset or hurt.

Some of the greatest empaths you will meet will stop at nothing to help an animal in distress or comfort a child. The fact is that empaths are also vulnerable. They know what it's like to have strong feelings which they cannot control. Additionally, they can relate to a defenseless animal that might be in pain or in need. So, they don't just say "oh, poor thing" and leave it at that. They will try their best to remedy the situation. If you find that you cannot stand anyone harming and animal or a child, then you are on the right track.

You don't just feel others' emotions, you also share their physical discomforts

There is a term called "sympathy pain" meaning that one person "feels" what another person is feeling when they are ill. This is common in married couples, parents and children, or siblings. Yet, truly empathetic people are able to sense what others are actually feeling when they are in pain or when they are ill.

Now, this isn't just a superficial reaction such as, "oh, that's gotta hurt!" This is a deep understanding of what the other person is going through. As a result, an empath may begin to feel physical discomfort mirroring what someone else is going through.

This reaction is not some kind of magical superpower. In fact, it is a logical reaction on the part of the brain. When an empath sees that another person has an illness, for example they have a cold, the empath's brain processes emotions in such a way that it begins to process its own feelings of physical discomfort mimicking the illness itself. While there is nothing actually wrong with the empath, the empath's brain begins to believe they are sick, too.

In most cases, empaths will simply begin to feel upset when they encounter people and animals in distress. Most empaths report feelings of dizziness, nausea and headaches when they encounter people and animals in distress. These feelings often go away when the person in question receives medical attention or when the empath is removed from the situation. But if the empath does not see that the person in pain has been tended to, the feelings may still linger for a while.

Intimate relationships can become overwhelming

Intimate relationships can take on various facets. For instance, we could be talking about a romantic relationship or a very close friendship. Regardless of the nature of the relationship itself, getting very close to someone can become overwhelming at times due to the emotion connection and bond that is developed.

The bond between two people, or perhaps as part of a group setting, can get pretty intense especially depending on the circumstances surrounding that relationship. Examples of this can be seen all over. For instance, you might find yourself developing a very close bond with survivors of a disaster or perhaps working with abuse victims. One classic example is the bond that teammates of sports teams develop. Teammates get to be so close that the bond they share lasts a lifetime. Similarly, firefighters and police officers also form tight-knit groups.

As a result, the emotions felt by one member of the team can spread like wildfire. If one member happens to be going through a tough time, then that emotion can blast through the entire crew. Empaths in particular may become overwhelming to a degree where their focus and attention will almost entirely focus on their mates even to the point of self-detriment.

Ideally, empaths are able to balance the load so that they are able to cope with the circumstances surrounding them. That way, they can still offer support to their friends and mates, but also stay grounded and not be hurt in the process.

You can't understand selfish people
Empaths are unable to wrap their minds around anyone who is selfish. This perception is due to the fact that empaths almost always put others ahead of themselves. As such, being selfish is something that an empath simply cannot comprehend.

In fact, a selfish individual is, in many ways, diametrically opposed to an empath. A selfish person neglects others' feelings and needs in order to put their own needs first. This attitude generally means that a selfish person will achieve their aims at the expense of others. In order to be that ruthless, a selfish person needs to completely disregard the emotions, needs and wants of others. As such, this lack of empathy allows selfish individuals to get their way regardless of the cost.

Furthermore, a lack of empathy is one of the core traits of psychopaths. An individual with a psychopathic personality usually finds themselves completely ignoring what someone else might be feeling. This leads them to commit heinous acts of violence simply because they cannot identify with their victims in any way.

While psychopaths may seem a bit extreme in this case, the underlying psychological theory stands on its own. That is why an empath is prone to self-sacrifice. This trait has been evidenced throughout our discussion thus far though we haven't quite articulated it in that manner until now. So, if you are prone to putting the needs of others ahead of your own, then you might very well be a true empath.

Throughout this chapter, we have highlighted the main attitudes of an empath. It is safe to say that you have checked off many boxes while leaving a few of them blank. If you find that you lack in some of these areas, then now is a good time to reflect on the ways in which you can improve your overall skills. After all, this book is intended to help you find the right path that will lead you to sharpen your empathetic skills. While some folks are more naturally empathetic than others, all of these skills require honing and development. So, now is the time to make a conscious choice to build up your skills and continue on the path to becoming a better person.

Chapter 4: Indigo Children

In the 1970s a parapsychologist, noticed an uprise of children born with a different aura. An aura is a field of energy that surrounds a person, certain people that can see auras see the different types of energy in colors. This parapsychologist noticed that a lot of children were being born with dark blue-violet or indigo auras. This color aura usually means a connection with a more spiritual self. She also noticed that these children were very different.

These children, thought different, they really felt more than they thought. This was such a phenomenon, there have even been rumors that the United States and Russian government took some of these children into a facility and conducted psychological tests on them. Now I don't know if that is true or not but this was not long after we had other psychological experiments conducted by our government, remote viewing, wind talkers, telekinetic experiments, etc.

Throughout the eighties, nineties, and into the new millennium more of these children have surfaced. These have been called Indigo children. Indigo children are believed to possess special, unusual, and sometimes supernatural traits and/or abilities. They have also been called "crystal children" or "star children". Indigos are here to help us recognize our true essence. We think that our minds and bodies are separate but the truth is they are not. Our DNA is changing, our brain waves are spontaneously moving into higher vibrational patterns, and little by little the human race is realizing there is something "more" and a lot are starting to move toward the thought pattern of "sentient beings".

Indigo children know there is something more and they have an inner knowledge that far exceeds our own. They sometimes travel between worlds at night when they are asleep, because that is how they gain their guidance and knowledge even if it is on an unconscious or even subconscious level. They know that our thoughts and our feelings are not really our own but rather an inner knowledge that is ancient and within us all placed there by a higher being.

You see thousands of years ago we began to think rather than feel. Even though the ability to "tap" into the collective conscious is still in all of us, we've forgotten how to do it or worse yet how to use it. Over time we gave our power to intellect which made us fearful, causing us to lose our divine connection to the collective consciousness and making us feel alone and hopeless.

Most academic scholars and psychologists see fit to label the indigos as ADD, ADHD, or ODD or with some other mental illness, anti-social or something along those lines.

They attempt to medicate them because they feel they are just dysfunctional. When Indigos take Ritalin or other psychotropic drugs they tend to lose touch with their intuition and psychic abilities, and their warrior personalities.

Many Indigos end up being home schooled and so the authorities label them as raised by narcissists and they are therefore considered in most cases as being emotionally abused. However, some say there is a link between Indigo children and autistic children; due to the fact that the autism rates have risen dramatically in the last twenty years and autistic children do tend to function on the extreme end of another spectrum.

Indigo children all share similar traits these include:
Most are born between 1978 and the present time.
They are headstrong
They are very creative

They unfortunately are prone to addictions, because of the lack of understanding by "normal" society and the fact they are drugged at such a young age

They are "old souls" meaning they have a wisdom and a knowledge that surpasses their physical ages

They have a deep desire to help the world in a big way

They are easily bored

They are prone to insomnia, nightmares, and some are fearful of falling asleep

They have a history of depression and even suicidal thoughts because they feel so alone, and are told all their lives they are not normal and are weird

They seek and want real, deep, and lasting friendships

They easily bond with plants and animals

They are often physically beautiful and have deep, penetrating eyes

They can entertain themselves, and play in their own world for hours, usually even having imaginary playmates

They love dolphins and fairies

They are empathic, curious, and strong willed

They have a very clear sense of purpose and self

They have a strong, subconscious sense of spirituality and this may not mean an organized religion

They sometimes have a feeling of entitlement

They have high IQs

They have a great intuitive ability

They will resist rigid authority they have no response to guilt, fear, or manipulation based disciplines. They know that we are all created equally and they will rebuke any authority that says different even to the point of anger sometimes.

Indigo children are here to help us on the path to love, brotherhood, unity, integrity, and they know it. They will stop at nothing to achieve what they are sent here to achieve. They are sometimes called "Natural children in an unnatural world". They have a distinct purpose and they will achieve it, they are here in strong numbers and the "rainbow children" that are succeeding them are coming in full force as well. They know that the time for awakening and ascension is now and they are here to usher us into this new age.

Chapter 5: The Benefits Of Using

Manipulation

As we have been talking about so far in this guidebook, there are a lot of different scenarios that you may use manipulation, and there are a lot of effects that can happen as a process as well, depending on how the manipulation is used. While we often think of manipulation as a bad thing, but there are actually quite a few benefits that are going to come with using manipulation in order to get what we want.

Just because we are getting what we want doesn't mean that we are going to always harm someone else. And this is the difference between regular manipulation and what is known as dark manipulation. It is an important distinction that we need to make. With regular manipulation, we want to get something, but we don't want the other person to get harmed or hurt in any manner, whether it is physical, mental, or emotional.

On the other hand, when it comes to dark manipulation, it isn't going to matter to the manipulator whether the other person gets harmed or not. They don't really care how much that person is harmed, and usually, there is going to be some kind of harm in the process. As long as the manipulator gets the thing that they want, they are going to be happy about the situation.

With that said, whether you are using manipulation in order to progress your own agenda while helping others (like in sales or getting some help on a group project), or you are using it to benefit yourself and you don't care if someone gets harmed in the process, there are going to be some benefits that come with using manipulation on a regular basis. Some of the benefits you can look for will include:

Manipulation is often going to work. The idea here is that if I know what I want and I know how to evoke a feeling in the other person so that they are more likely to do what I want, then manipulation is going to be effective, and we are able to measure this effect as well. Think of how this works. Businesses are going to spend billions of dollars in research to do various marketing strategies to point to how well the manipulation that is found in their campaigns and their advertisements work, so we know that manipulation must be something that works.

Of course, you have to do things the right way. it is not enough to just put an ad online or on television and assume people are going to come in droves to purchase the product. There is just too much competition out there, and often we see so many advertisements that it is impossible to just see something and be manipulated by it. There has to be another level, and there needs to be some experience and expertise to pull it off, and that is what the research dollars of many companies are spending on.

The same idea can be said when we take a look at regular manipulation that an individual is going to use. It is not enough for us to walk up to someone and say, "Do what I want!" The target is likely going to take a look at us and just laugh and walk away. And you would do the same as well. You need to make sure that you are using the right techniques, and that you really understand what the other person will respond to. When you use manipulation in the right manner though, and with the right techniques you will find that it actually works which is a really cool benefit.

The next benefit that comes with manipulation is the idea that we can become pretty good at it. In fact, as you went over the previous chapter, it is likely that you saw at least a few times when you have used manipulation in the past to help you get what you wanted, even if the answers ended up surprising you in the process. This manipulation is actually something that we have been practicing since before we were able to walk.

This is because there was a time when we were not able to talk, and we still needed to get things. We needed food something to drink to feel loved to have clothes, to get baths to get diapers changed and more. Even though we were not able to talk and voice our opinions on our own, and we were not able to take care of these things on own at this time, we were able to use manipulation in order to influence mom and dad to do the work for us.

Since we have been able to read others since a young age in order to help us get what we wanted as a baby up through adulthood, we are already good at reading others, often much better than we would think. And we can even find that, with a bit of practice, we are able to quickly guess the right thing to do to help us motivate that other person in the process as well. Of course, some of us are going to be much better at doing this than others, but it is still something that we can work on to improve and see some great results with influencing others.

Easier to get what we want. If you decided to come right out and ask the other person to give you exactly what you wanted, it is likely that they are going to say no. if you just ask about it, without using any of the techniques that we will discuss in this guidebook and the techniques of manipulation, then the other person really has no need to help you and won't feel guilty about doing something that they have no interest in helping out with.

However, if you are able to use some of the manipulation tools and techniques that we have been discussing so far, and you are able to trigger some feelings in the other person, you will find that it is easier to get the other person to do what you want. They are going to feel some kind of obligation in order to help you, even if they are not sure what that is all about. And even if they are not fond of the idea of helping out with it, they are more likely to say yes.

This is going to be really great news for you. It means that you are going to be able to get the other person to say yes to what you want them to, without having to push too hard or worry as much about whether they are going to say yes or no to you. You will have already put in the work that is needed to convince them to work with you, and it is likely, especially if you spent time analyzing them and using the right technique for their needs, that they are going to agree to what you want.

And the final benefit that we are going to take a look at here when it comes to using manipulation and some of the different techniques that come with it is the idea of power. Since all relationships whether they are with family, at work, or an intimate relationship, are going to have some element of power in them. All of us would like to have power over others or at least over someone at some point, and manipulation is going to be the tool that we need to ensure that we gain that power over our target.

Now, there are those who will take that power and go too far. This is where the manipulation is going to turn into abuse and some other problems as well. But the power that comes with manipulation can sometimes be as simple as having a bit of control over one person in your life, even your child, and it doesn't always have to be an abusive or negative kind of thing to work with.

The negatives of manipulation

Of course, there have to be a few negatives that come with manipulation. If there weren't, then everyone would use this technique all of the time and we wouldn't have some of the negative connotations that come with it along the way either. The negatives of this are going to mainly occur when you are not versed well enough in using manipulation or if someone catches you in the act of manipulating them. We will explore these a bit more as we get through these sections. Some of the different negatives that can come with using manipulation in your own life can include:

Manipulation is something that has the potential to backfire quite a bit. People are often going to have some kind of sense about when another person is trying to manipulate them. This is because we are heightened to the idea that because we want something out of another person, it is likely that someone else is going to want something out of us as well. When someone starts to sense that they are being manipulated, it is not going to end well for you and it is often going to generate a lot of anger, resentment and more.

If the target senses that the manipulator is trying to take control, or they feel that the manipulator is trying to take some power over them in a sneaky manner, it is likely that the target is not going to trust that person any longer. At this point, if the target feels like you have successfully manipulated them, they may withhold something from their manipulator in order to get even, even if it is not that big of a deal what you are trying to get. And if the target thinks that this manipulation has gone even further and feels like their feelings are being toyed with, then it is sure to bring out a big power struggle between the two people in this game, and the trust is going to head right out the window.

Another negative to be careful about is that we often are not going to think through the manipulation that we are doing before we do it. Before we even have a good idea of what we want out of the relationship, or before we start to evaluate the possibility of just coming out to the target and asking for what we want in a direct manner, we are going to head right over and start manipulating the other person.

The reason that we do this is because we are so eager to try out the techniques, we are eager to get what we want, or we just assume that the other person will say no to us and we don't want to worry about the rejection in the process. This step though is going to lead to some assumptions about you both that could end up corroding the relationship that you are in. remember that once the relationship is gone and corroded, it is impossible for you to regain the control that you need in order to manipulate that person again.

There are a lot of different indirect versions of manipulation that can come into play, and sometimes they will become almost a habit in the relationship. Some of these are going to include options like guilt tripping, abusive criticism, and complaining. And another layer of the power struggle is going to start showing up in the relationship when we use these techniques all of the time, even though that was usually not the intention.

The best way to avoid this kind of issue is to make sure that you don't jump into the manipulation too quickly. You need to be able to think it all through properly, and really consider when you will use it, how much you will use, how you will manipulate and more. Manipulation is something that has to be thought out, and if you are not ready to do that, then you are going to find that it is hard to keep control over your target.

And finally, there are some people who jump into the idea of manipulation in order to give them power, control, and everything that they imagined they ever wanted. And for some of these manipulators, that is exactly what they want and they couldn't be happier. On the other hand, there are some people who find that doing this manipulation is not going to give them what they want.

Think of it this way. Maybe you manipulated someone into a relationship with you and into saying they love you because you were looking for some attention and love from another person. You finally get into that relationship and get them to say those words. But it just isn't going to satisfy most people the way that they had hoped because they know that the other person was tricked into saying it. Yes, the target is going to say they did it on their own, but the manipulator knows the work they did behind the scenes to make those words come out. Sure, you technically got what you wanted out of the situation, but it just doesn't seem as satisfying when it is done this way.

As you can see here, there are a lot of different benefits that are going to come into play when it is time to use manipulation. And this is often why people will choose to work with manipulation in order to help them gain power, get control over someone else, and to get what they want out of life. But it is important to note that there are also going to be some negatives that come with manipulation, and it doesn't always work out the way that you would like. Understanding both sides of the story before you start to use these tools of manipulation can make a world of difference as well.

Chapter 6: Main Characteristics And

Archetypes

Like the empathic personality traits there are certain archetype's associated with the empath nature. These are the parts of psyche, soul and self which all empaths have the capability to possess. They also can be enhanced and evolved into a career or profession, and are simultaneously strongly associated with an empath's true purpose or path.

These archetypal beings are written as if you already identify with them. Each has a final paragraph to help you understand your own inner processes, subconscious workings and life experiences. Simultaneously, if you are not yet completely sure whether you embody these empath traits, the "practical implications" section can help you make sense of your potential gifts and strengths.

1.The Artist & Visionary

You are an artist. Due to your ability to connect to something above and beyond you through your deep and rich emotional wisdom and intuitive sight, you can also tune in to universal archetypes, ideas, concepts, and often ingenious images and thoughts in a unique way. This makes you a natural artist, creative and visionary. Whether you choose to express yourself through song, dance, art, painting, drawing, poetry, writing, photography, film making, or directing, you can achieve great things! The visionary aspect to your nature can, literally, connect on an unseen level to some concept or archetype beyond the physical realm, and further bring it forth into the physical. Alanis Morissette is one of the most well-known empaths and even if you have not yet heard of her, her music inspires many people around the world.

Practical Implications of being the Artist and Visionary: If you embody the artist, creative, or visionary you may have found yourself as a child daydreaming and letting your mind wander to unseen worlds and ideas. Your imagination was rich and you may have been bored in social or overly externally stimulating situations. You also may have naturally had a strong inner knowing that you could come up with better or ingenious ideas and solutions to ones being presented in school, or by your teachers and peers. Your abstract and creative ways of thinking may not have been appreciated or understood by others, yet you always maintained your faith in yourself.

2.The Creative Mind with Infinite Potential (Potential Careers or Paths: Musician, Performer or Storyteller)

Like the artist and visionary, you are highly creative and may be or become a musician, performer or storyteller. Even if you don't ground this into a career or profession, you still have strong elements of being a performer. Many people naturally assume that to be an empath means to be an introvert, yet they are not synergistic. Many empathic people are introverted as there are some strong intrinsic links and associations, however many empaths are also highly extroverted. This is because of your ability to connect and because of your love of connection. Once you find yourself, become centered and begin to live in an empathic and harmonious flow; you will find that using your gifts and personality strengths through poetry, performing, storyteller or by connecting others through musical expression comes naturally to you.

Practical Implications of being the Creative Mind with Infinite Potential: You found yourself naturally being able to play music, pick up a drum beat or understand aspects relating to advanced storytelling or performance without being taught. You had an ability to connect to others on a deep level, without teaching, and could easily and almost effortlessly pick up and adopt many roles. You may have related to characters in plays, performers, or musicians in a deeper way unexplained by your mind, and experienced certain music as a transcendental and "other-worldly" experience. Even as a child or teenager you were aware that you would "make it" in a big way and not sacrifice your dreams, hopes or aspirations, or integrity, for a career you simply had no enjoyment in doing. World- class artists, actors and actresses, authors, writers, performers, musicians, film directors and entertainers are not seen as above or unequal to you. To you, they are perfectly "normal" and legitimate career choices.

3.The Healer, Counselor or Therapist

Because of your unique gifts to connect to others on a deep level, you are a natural healer, counselor and therapist. Many empaths actually go onto becoming healers and therapists as these paths and professions are strongly associated with your true nature. As a healer, counselor, or therapist you possess vast levels of compassion, kindness and a genuine desire to help and be of service. You have a wise and empathic nature and are very patient, and with incredible listening skills. People feel comforted, safe and protected around you and you tend to live and resonate in your heart chakra. Your **heart chakra** is known as the central chakra, the energy vortex which links lower self and higher self. It is the seat of compassion, kindness, empathy, and a connection to others and the natural world, and having a strong heart chakra enables you to thrive in any healing or counseling profession. You also may be a healer or counselor to your friends and family.

Practical Implications of being the Healer, the Counselor, and the Therapist: You had a unique way of connecting to others on a deep level and may have found strangers coming up to you to talk when in your late teens to early 20s. People had an unexplainable pull to you and knew they could open up to you. You may have had a natural connection with animals and nature and felt most content and at peace in their presence, like you weren't being judged and could be yourself. You also may have been intrinsically drawn to quantum physics, eastern mythology or Buddhism books and had strong inner recognition of the significance of holistic health and alternative medicine.

4. The Animal Whisperer, Charity Worker, and Volunteer

The empath personality is defined by connection, understanding and being able to feel what it is like to be another. Many empaths take this ability further and can actually read minds, or at least merge with another on such a level that they know what they are thinking or feeling. This gift can be used in **animal whispering.** You are a sensitive soul with a big heart, therefore choosing a path or career aligned to helping animals and being a guide or channel for them is a route many empaths choose to take. You tend to feel more comfortable around animals or in nature where you can just be yourself. This is where you along with many empaths not only survive, but thrive. Simultaneously, many empaths choose to become involved in charity or animal welfare work so this is another direction which you may share a resonance. Essentially any hobby, career, path or direction allowing you to make use of your sensitive, caring, empathic and intuitive gifts will allow you to shine.

Practical Implications of being the Animal Whisperer, Charity Worker, and Volunteer: You may have developed a deep and personal relationship to animals which no one knew about. When visiting zoos, sanctuaries, wildlife areas or parks you could speak to animals on an inner level and felt an emotional and telepathic connection. When coming across a homeless person in the street you have had real and sincere compassion for them, which sometimes translated into pain. You may have also felt different from your family in some unexplainable way, like you were the black sheep, odd ball or lone wolf. You always had a deep empathy and compassion for those who appeared less fortunate than you or those in your family and close proximity.

5. The Spiritual Healer and Energy Worker

This brings us on to spirituality. You are deeply spiritual and intuitive, even if you are not yet conscious of it. This can manifest in many magical ways, such as knowing what someone is about to say before they say it, sensing an event about to occur, or being able to pull something out of someone hidden deep within. You may be psychic, have precognitive dreams or even visions and may live in an alternate reality together. Many empaths exist in multiple dimensions with one foot in this world and the other in another; this allows you to connect with a higher source or power. Whether you call this god, the goddess, spirit, or the universe, it is very real to you and when **tuning in** to connect to these realms you can be a powerful and unique asset in someone's life. You may use your spiritual gifts and awareness to write books, heal others, teach in some way, or take on a leadership role. Mother Teresa is a prime example of a spiritual empath who used her gifts in service to others. Energy healing or the mystic arts come naturally to you and, like the natural counselor and caregiver, you may find people gravitating towards you for advice, compassion or perspective. You also have a *healing nature*- others feel better just being in your presence.

Practical Implications of being the Spiritual Healer and Energy Worker: You were deeply drawn to all thing mystical, spiritual and metaphysical from your mid to late teens. You may have been interested in quantum physics, crystals, astrology, supernatural abilities, and ancient wisdom. You possessed a deep knowing of all things and could see beyond people's hidden motives, feelings, and intentions. You also may have begun meditating at a young age, and reading spiritual literature or wisdom infused books on the occult, spiritual or metaphysical topics. Your dreams may have been vast and profound and you may have naturally begun to astral project or lucid dream. All of your senses become heightened and your love for animals and mother earth increased with the more knowledge you acquired.

6. The Carer, Social or Support Worker, or Elderly Companion

Connected to being a natural healer, counselor and therapist is your inner tendencies to taking on a caring and supporting role. Many of the caregivers, social and support workers, and companions you see today are either empaths or have strong empathic tendencies. Unlike other characters and personality types, such as narcissists or energy vampires who thrive from taking from others, you thrive from giving and taking on a supportive and caring role. This is essential because of your ability and need for connection. As an empath, you are deeply connected to your environments, surroundings and other people (and animals), and anything which threatens your connection can lead to pain, struggle, and inner turmoil. As we explored, this is why it is essential to protect yourself and develop healthy boundaries, and why channeling and expressing these qualities of yours can lead to you living your best and most happy and harmonious life!

Practical Implications of being the Carer, the Social or Support Worker, or Companion: Growing up you may have been particularly shy and introspective, and perhaps told you were too sensitive, more often than not. This is because you are extremely compassionate and naturally destined to help others in some way, and take on a caring and supporting role. As a child and teenager, you may not have understood this and therefore became shy and quiet as a result. You also may have had strong feelings of wanting to be a vet or the like when asked what you want to be when you are older. Finally, you may have had a strong aversion to violence and became increasingly disturbed when seeing violent or 'hateful' acts and scenes on television or in movies, or when witnessing the suffering of others.

7. The Dreamer, Seer, and Psychic

One thing that is not often taught in schools nor accepted mainstream is the fact that you, dear empath, are an extremely gifted person. You are a dreamer- you love to explore your dreams and merge with other worlds. Yet your abilities to merge with the subconscious also lies beyond this. Many empaths have a **seer**-like quality to them because, as stated, you can connect to some archetype or invisible symbol or idea which transcends the three-dimensional reality. In addition to actually dreaming and enjoying the world of dreams, you also may have the ability to astral travel, astral project, or lucid dream at will. These are three things which come naturally to many empaths and when you are young you may not be able to explain them. We all have an astral body, an energetic layer of ourselves which extends beyond the physical. This astral layer of existence is responsible for all links and connections to psychic, intuitive, spiritual, and archetypal phenomena. It is also where you can connect to dream worlds and your subconscious during sleep or in that period between waking life and sleep when you are in between the worlds.

Practical Implications of being the Dreamer, Seer, and the Psychic: You often had dreams you couldn't explain yet knew were sending you a message or direct insight in some way. You knew this even before reading and learning about what was occurring. If you embody these empath aspects you also have a deep inner feeling regarding people and places. You would "just know" if somewhere didn't feel right or a person didn't have good energy. You also would know which way to go and which route was the best when on an adventure, exploration, or nature walk. Your dreams may have been vivid and you may even have found yourself become bolted out of or into your body from sleep.

8. The Independent Worker and 'Self-Employed One'

Because of your inherent dislike of certain characters, roles, interactions, and energies you are most suited to self-employment or highly independent roles. This can manifest in a number of ways, such as through being a self- employed plumber, electrician, handywoman or man or owning your own small business. The main point with this is that you have an aversion and furthermore extreme sensitivity to certain noises which come with 'normal' jobs. Working in an office, for example, can be extremely stressful and even harmful to your empathic nature, as can working in sales or any job where you have to interact with a large number of people on a daily basis. You prefer to work in a creative, healing or service- oriented role, or at least a job which allows you to daydream, connect to your own inner empathy, and not be destructive or harmful to others or in the environment.

Practical Implications of being the Independent Worker and Self- Employed One: You had a particular aversion in school to certain topics and perspectives taught as truth. You were not necessarily an outward rebel but you were an inward one, and frequently went against the norm. Structure and oppressive ways made you feel limited and you preferred to come up with your own creative solutions and ways of thinking than following set orders. Rules and regulations may have seemed oppressive to you and your political views may have been strongly steered towards liberalism. All in all, traditional roles, paths and your "9 to 5" never resonated.

Although these are not different types of empath, becoming aware of the varying aspects to the empath personality and your nature can really aid in your journey of discovery and self- development. Empathy is an encompassing gift and its applications are vast. Understanding yourself and the various archetypes of the "empath characteristics" may just be the key to your own personal puzzle!

Chapter 7: Start With Yourself

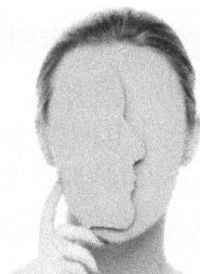

Empaths are naturally disposed to the healing arts, and often feel a compulsive need to help others. But no one, no matter how deeply empathic, can be an effective healer for others if they aren't willing to invest some of that healing power into themselves, first. To become an empowered empath, you'll need to take some steps to examine your own emotional and physical wounds, work on self-healing, and build enough self-love to stay invested in caring for yourself before others for the rest of your life. This is easier said than done, but it is absolutely necessary. No doctor can perform surgery if they refuse to let their own broken fingers heal. The time and energy you spend on self-healing will pay off in the long run, as it will automatically inspire others to trust in your judgment and value your opinions as deeply as you value them yourself.

Who Are You, Really?
Empaths don't only absorb the emotions, energies, or physical sensations of others. We also take on thoughts, preferences, opinions, and value structures. Many of us spend so much time during our developmental years enmeshed with other people that we have a hard time understanding what we truly think, like, or believe in, ourselves, without the context of our community, friends, family, or work environment to tell us what we **should** be thinking.
One of the first, and most important, steps in your healing journey is to rediscover your core identity. Your core identity is the

person that you are without any of the decorations that society places upon us all. If you woke up tomorrow without a career, a bank account, a group of friends, a social media following, a home, a car, a grocery list, a schedule, or a set of responsibilities... what would you do with yourself? How would you choose to spend your time? How would you behave?

Most of us display our core identities in early childhood but quickly lose touch with them as we age and begin to worry about things like our future careers, our sexual identities, or our social popularity. So in order to get back in touch with this part of ourselves, we have to work methodically on peeling back some of our layers. Here we have a step by step guide to getting back to your authentic identity as an adult. The steps can certainly be altered and tailored to suit your personal needs—this is by no means the only way to reconnect with your core identity, but simply an outline to use as a jumping-off point. In this process, it's also important to listen to your gut and follow your instincts to see where they may lead. Don't allow someone else's guidelines to take precedent over your instincts—after all, no one can ever know you as well as you know yourself.

1- *Take some time for yourself* - This may prove challenging, but in order to begin this journey, you'll need to find some alone time in a space where you won't be interrupted or distracted. This could be a retreat or solo vacation, but if time or finances are tight, there is plenty of easily accessible alternatives. This alone time doesn't necessarily need to last more than a few hours, and can be done in the privacy of your own home--through getting some distance from items that remind you of your constructed identity is recommended, if possible. Go for a walk in the park, or a hike; make arrangements to pet-sit for a friend whose home is less familiar; spend an afternoon at a comfortable table in your favorite café; camp in your own back yard for a night;

you could even convert a room in your home into a temporary sanctuary space, draping sheets or scarves over furniture and hiding away photos, tchotchkes, and anything that reminds you of your work life or chores. The point is to break your routine and get a little mental space away from the stressors of your usual daily life.

2- *Find some stillness* – Even when we are alone, in a sanctuary space or nature, most of us are accustomed to constant activity when we are awake. We play with our smartphones and computers; we watch television, we eat mindlessly, we fidget; this inability to be quiet and still is a modern symptom of chronic anxiety that exists on a culture-wide scale. It is one of the primary reasons why some people find meditation arduous. These days, we're all receiving constant reminders that we aren't enough on our own—that we need to be earning more, doing more, owning more; that we need to be busier and more productive and better informed so that we might stand a chance at being happier. In order to reconnect with your authentic self, you need to learn how to silence the voice in your head that wants you to believe you're wasting your time if you aren't doing something with it. Thinking and feeling are both important things to do with our time, and when we are always acting, consuming, or creating, we don't give ourselves nearly enough time or space to do either.

3- *Make a list* – This may sound silly, but I'd urge you to take this part of the process seriously. Once you've gotten some distance from your social and professional spheres, and spent some quiet time on your own, start making a list for yourself, with two columns: one for the things in your life that make you happy, and another for the things that make you angry, sad, or stand in the way of your happiness. Try to remain emotionally objective as you write this list, especially for the column of unhappy realities; you don't want to focus on the negative or pour too much energy into self-pity or the blame game. Also, do your best, to be honest with yourself about these lists—it doesn't matter what other people think you **should** be happy or sad about, what matters is how you actually feel. Your friends and family might think that a happy marriage is the most important goal and that you should be over the moon with your committed partner—but if the relationship isn't working for you, their judgments will never be enough to make you truly happy. Avoid thinking in terms of comparison as much as possible; another person's version of happiness may look and feel completely different than your own.

4- *Honest self-reflection* – This is often the hardest part of the process, so it's perfectly fine to take a break before this step and come back to it when you have plenty of energy and enthusiasm to pour into it. First, evaluate your two-column list, and ask yourself some questions. How might you bring the items in your "happy" column into your life on a more consistent basis? How might you shield yourself from the things that make you unhappy? How many of these things are within your control? How many are up to other people? How many are up to nature and divine energies? How many of the things in the "unhappy" column are actually **good** for you (like exercise, or sleep)? How many of the things in the "happy" column are detrimental to your well-being, in the long run? Are some of the items in opposite columns feeding into each other in a cyclical way, perhaps? And how many of the things that make you "unhappy" are things you invited—or still continue to invite—into your life yourself? There are no right or wrong answers here, and plenty of other probing questions to ask. The real point, though, is to try and get a sense of how much power you truly hold over your own happiness. Many people feel as though they are at the mercy of the world—that things happen to them, and their only option is to react. In truth, though, we are all able to make choices that invite happiness in and shield us from unneeded sources of anxiety and negativity. Pain is a part of life, and can't be avoided completely, but there is a great difference between processing inevitable pain, and feeding into your own chronic suffering. While it may be initially painful to reflect on some of this list, it will ultimately serve to highlight some important truths, such as: How much of your energy is spent serving your happiness, and how much is spent on feeding other peoples' satisfaction? How much of your unhappiness is due to the guilt, frustration, resentment, or shame that comes after making poor choices? Remember, this isn't a time for self-flagellation; self-awareness is our primary goal. Everyone makes poor choices sometimes. Try to forgive yourself; it's the first step in moving forward and breaking unhealthy patterns.

5- *Get creative and playful* – After the previous step, you may be feeling a bit raw, vulnerable, emotional, anxious, or frustrated with yourself. If so, you'll want to throw yourself into a drastic change right away. But before you do anything impulsive, try to take some time to remind yourself of your strengths. Creative expression is one of many excellent ways to do this; it helps us to practice resourcefulness, to think outside the box, to take chances, to work on problem-solving in a way that's enjoyable rather than stressful; furthermore, it can help give us more insight into the inner workings of our souls, helping deeply repressed emotions and thoughts to rise to the surface, and reminding us to listen to our own instincts. If you don't identify as a particularly creative person, you can still gain a lot from the practice of free-journaling, for instance, or dabbling in artistic endeavors without the intention of ever showcasing your work. You can also express creativity through cooking, gardening, or woodworking, for example. Whatever you choose, simply keep in mind that your goal is to find something that allows you to be playful—to be creative without worrying about what is right or wrong, without deadlines, without comparing your creation to someone else's. You want to create in the same way that children do, removing self-doubt and anxiety from the equation. This way, the things you create will be authentic projections of your core identity. If you are a painter, for instance, you may note that the paintings you make for yourself feature different color schemes or stylistic elements, as compared to those you create for an audience.

6- *Make an action plan* – This step can be a constantly evolving process; there's no need to rush it or put a strict deadline on any aspect of your personal growth. However, it is important to start making some concrete plans to move forward that will help to invite more authentic joy into your life and break negative cycles. This may mean taking steps to change your career, spending more time on a hobby or recreational activity that you've previously neglected, or working to remove yourself from relationships that take your energy away from your happiness. You might aim to start small, perhaps by incorporating five minutes of meditation into your daily routine, or you might feel ready to do something more extreme, such as picking up and moving to a warmer, sunnier climate. Whatever choice you make, be prepared for some pushback; it usually takes more than one person to keep a routine in place, and the things that are making you unhappy might actually be working really well for the other people in your life. Acknowledge feelings like fear, guilt, or obligation, but try not to let them rule you. It can be immensely helpful to work through those feelings with a therapist or emotional coach.

7- *Rewrite your personal story* – This can be difficult to do with people who've already known you for a long time, but one deeply empowering step in this process is to work on describing yourself differently when introduced to new acquaintances. As an example, an empathic aspiring author who has spent years around people who invalidate their talents might introduce themselves in a self-deprecating way, describing their day job as "just something I do to pay the bills." But when they begin to validate their authentic identity by confidently telling others: "I am a writer," they'll begin to rewire their own thought patterns and change not only the way they look at themselves but also the way they are perceived by others. They'll automatically feel empowered to invest more time and energy into their craft, and project a level of authenticity that will persuade others to take them seriously as a writer. This same theory can apply to all sorts of situations; a person leaving an abusive relationship, for instance, might rewrite their personal story to describe themselves as a "survivor" rather than as a "victim." A stay-at-home dad might choose to describe himself as "a caregiver **and** a mathematician." Finally, this process doesn't need to be centered on career identities or family roles. One beautiful and transformative experience is to proudly declare, for the first time, that you are an empath, first and foremost.

Learning to Listen to Your Body
Our modern society places a great deal of value on intellect, practicality, and rationality. Most of us receive hundreds of implicit messages daily from the media, economic marketplace, and even our communities, reminding us that our thoughts should be honored over our feelings or emotions. Often, we are told that our feelings are invalid if we cannot find a rational way to explain or justify them. For example, a person who is dissatisfied in a romantic relationship may

be advised by magazine articles, television shows, and even their family or friends, to remain involved with their partner unless they can cite a rational explanation for their dissatisfaction. They may be repeatedly asked what their partner has done wrong or encouraged to reconsider their feelings if the partner does not "deserve" to be broken up with. What this person may not be asked, however, is whether or not they feel good about who they are within the context of the relationship; whether they feel a spark or a sense of sentimentality for their partner, or if they simply feel bored and anxious around them.

Too frequently, we become so preoccupied with our thoughts that we forget actually to experience our feelings. Our emotional and physical bodies are both very wise and will work hard to protect us from things that drain or damage us. Even if our minds can't find a legitimate reason to object to certain circumstances in our lives, our bodies will consistently work to clue us into the fact that something needs to change.

Mindfulness meditation is one of the easiest ways to get back into the habit of listening to our bodies. Talk therapy can also be immensely helpful if you find yourself struggling in this area. Those of us who grow up in emotionally repressed environments may have a difficult time deciphering the difference between a feeling and a thought, or in naming specific emotions; there is no shame in this, so long as you are willing to seek guidance from others and work to be conscious of your own feelings.

Chapter 8: You Can Achieve Mindful

Relationships Too

Effective communication is one of the most valuable skills that you can build, and it is going to be one of the most useful in helping you achieve the mindful relationships that you want. In both your professional and personal life, it is the connections that you're able to make which will give you a leg up in any situation. Even more so in a professional context when managers and leaders are always on the lookout for employees with the right communication skills who can articulate themselves well enough to be able to work well with others in order to achieve the common goals which have been set. Even the best-laid plans can quickly unravel when poor communication is present.

Understanding the roadblocks that prevent effective communication requires just as much effort as it does in working on developing effective communication techniques and skills. If not dealt with, these barriers which you either consciously or subconsciously form can still prevent your message from coming across as clearly as it otherwise should be. To open the lines of communication and prevent any barriers from further standing in your way requires a combination of *both* skills and the ability to understand and overcome the obstacles that will prevent your message from coming through loud and clear.

Let's dive into the common communication obstructions that you might encounter in your everyday communication:

Perceptions - Your perceptions are the barriers you create in your mind that stops you from communicating as well as you could be. Perceptions, preconceived notions, assumptions and bias are factors that lead to typical misunderstandings if the person you're talking to was trying to gauge how you feel based on your body language. Yes, your perceptions are going to affect you on a subconscious level, and this is going to translate into your body language, even when you think you may be doing a good job of hiding it. There's a difference between someone who's communicating with an open mind and someone who is not. The open-minded individual will reflect this in their body language, which will mimic the way they feel by maintaining an open posture and expressing interest in the conversation by leaning forward and maintaining good eye contact. Someone who is not communicating with an open mind, on the other hand, is going to be closed off and reflect this in their posture by finding it difficult to keep good eye contact, crossing their arms in front of their chest or have their body angled away from the speaker, signaling their disinterest.

Emotions - Your emotions can act as a barrier, and the way that you feel during a conversation is going to have an impact on how well you receive messages and how well you're able to articulate yourself. Think of a time when you were not in the right emotional state, perhaps you were upset or distressed by something that happened earlier. In walks a colleague and tries to discuss something important that happened. You may be nodding along and agreeing in all the right places, but you're not really listening because you're still too wound up and replaying the events that happened a few hours ago in your mind. A few hours later, you've already forgotten half of what your colleague was trying to tell you. Now, think of a time when you were completely focused, motivated and energized and your colleague tried to talk to you again about an important workplace issue. In this different emotional state, your motivation is likely to make you more focused, and you're listening attentively, absorbing every detail of what's being said to you. A few hours later, that information is still fresh in your mind, and perhaps you're even feeling energized enough to want to expand on your colleagues' ideas and make it better. Notice what different emotions can make in the same situation. Emotions sometimes have a way of taking over when we don't know how to regulate them well. In a highly emotional state, it is easy to let our judgments be clouded and affected by the way that we feel at the time we're making the decision. Emotional intelligence is fast becoming a prized skill to possess, along with effective communication, as more people start to realize the importance of being able to keep your emotions in check and learn how to regulate them so they no longer act as a hindrance towards effective communication.

The Physical Obstructions - Many office setups these days tend to favor open floor plans because it allows communication between colleagues to happen efficiently and quickly. Physical barriers like cubicles or doors create a divide and separation between people and even though you might not be thinking twice about it, these barriers are preventing you from communicating effectively. Imagine trying to talk to your colleague and having to peer uncomfortable over the cubicle just to contact them. Or even standing behind the cubicle divider as you attempt to have a conversation. Whether you realize it or not, the presence of these physical barriers makes a difference. The next time you're trying to have a conversation with a colleague, observe how it feels when there's nothing standing between you and how it feels when there's a divide. Conversations seem to flow a lot better when two people can openly observe each other's physical cues and facial expressions without the distraction of having a barrier in between.

Genders - We united as we can be, we're also divided into certain areas, gender being one of them. We may all be human, but men and women can operate very differently on so many aspects that sometimes these differences become communication barriers. Even though workplace communication has come a long way compared to what it was a few years ago, the difference in the style of communicating between genders can still be a cause for a breakdown and cause problems and misunderstandings. Overcoming this barrier, however, is easy enough when everyone remembers to be respectful of each other's opinions and ideas.

Culture - We live in an age where we have become a global community, especially in business and educational environments. People from all walks of life, across different backgrounds and cultures, are now merging together in more situations, particularly in the workplace. While globalization has no doubt introduced a lot of new opportunities, it has also brought with it a potential communication barrier when we fail to understand and be mindful of cultural sensitivities. Respecting the values and beliefs of different cultures is required for effective communication to happen, along with the willingness to be able to adapt to the needs of others. There may be times when you might be required to make the necessary adjustments out of respect for someone else's culture, and it is your willingness to accommodate these differences which will determine how well the communication process flows.

Languages - Along with cultural barriers, language is another barrier that you might have to contend with as part of being a globalized society. Different cultures would naturally have their own language, and with that comes the different accents that we need to contend with. At times, the way a person speaks might prove to be a barrier if others have a hard time understanding what they're trying to say. Examples of language barriers might be speech impediments or the use of different jargon, accents we don't always recognize and even the speed at which someone else is talking might prove to be a challenge when it comes to comprehending what they're trying to say.

A Lack of Confidence and Self-Esteem - The way that you feel about yourself can act as a potential communication barrier if it affects your ability to articulate yourself. A lack of self-confidence and low levels of self-esteem can prevent you from making a connection with others. Being cautious or even afraid to speak out will make you feel isolated and removed, and others might start to view you as antisocial if it seems like you're trying to avoid communication when really the truth is that you're simply not confident enough to express your ideas.

Barriers That Prevent Effective Listening

Active listening is very much a part of the communication process, and like verbal communication, there are barriers or roadblocks that often stand in the way and prevent active listening from taking place:

Too Much Information - Information overload is real, and being bombarded with too much information all at once prevents active listening from taking place. When you're feeling overwhelmed and your emotions start to take over, concentrating becomes harder, and when you're struggling to keep up with everything that you're hearing, that sense of frustration makes it even harder to retain your focus. All that's happening when there's information overload is that you keep falling further behind.

Being Too Focused on Your Own Agenda - When all you can think about is your own agenda, you're going to have a hard time concentrating on what someone else is saying because you're going to be too busy formulating a response in your mind. Remember how multitasking is not possible in ineffective communication? How would you be able to fully pay attention to what someone is saying when your mind is distracted by trying to come up with the perfect reply.

Physical Distractions - Even the way that you feel physically has an impact on your listening abilities. When you're healthy and energetic, active listening is a lot easier compared to if you were feeling poorly or ill. If you're not physically okay, consider rescheduling the conversation to another time when you're able to give the speaker your undivided attention.

External Noises - Sometimes, the distractions don't come from within you, or from the speaker. The distractions instead could come from the external noises all around you, depending on where you're having your conversation. Needless to say, a distracting and noisy environment is not going to be very conducive to an effective and engaging conversation. It's hard to pay attention when there are a lot of other things going on around you. Picking the right environment for your discussion is just as important as picking the right time to talk.

Being Critical - It cannot be emphasized enough how important it is to have a conversation with an open mind. The moment you're critical or biased towards the speaker, part of your brain is already shut off to the conversation even before it has had a chance to properly take place. Instead of listening attentively to the speaker, you're going to be too busy being critical or thinking about all the flaws you can spot, and you lose sight of the importance of the message they were trying to convey.

Being Too Emotional - Nothing snatches your focus and distracts you quite as quickly as intense emotions do.

Sometimes, the words or phrases that a speaker might use could spark an intense emotional reaction within us. Whether we feel happy, excited, frustrated, sad or angry and what's being said, these emotions have one thing in common. They're distracting us from actively listening to what the speaker is trying to say.

Other Barriers Which Prevent Effective Communication

Aside from the physical and emotional barriers which could stand in the way of effective communication, other obstacles that need to be overcome for the betterment of your communication skills include:

Not Having Enough Time - Being pressed for time is a barrier that has become all too common these days. It's happening more and more as our lives seem to get busier, and we constantly seem to be in a race against time to get everything done in a day that needs to. Not having enough time to stop and pay attention long enough is no doubt an obstacle that stops effective communication from taking place.

Avoiding the Act of Stereotyping - Your perceptions can distort not just the way you see things, but the way that you perceive others too. A flaw in our human nature is a tendency to only see what we want to see, forming impressions and assumptions based on the small amounts of information that we receive, or basing it on past experiences we might have encountered. Generalizing and stereotyping others could lead to false assumptions and prevent you from listening to their point of view in the open-minded manner that you should.

Assuming Others Feel the Same Way - Tell five people the same piece of information and you'll be met with five different conclusions. This happens because the information is received and interpreted differently, and just because you might be actively listening, it doesn't mean everyone else is. Assuming everyone is going to arrive at the same conclusions as you become a barrier when it stops you from seeking clarification and acting on what you believe may be right. The communication process can only be considered successful when the message has been explicitly and clearly received by all five people involved in the conversation. The safest bet is to always seek clarity while making your own views known to others.

Leaping to Your Own Conclusions - Assumptions are not the only obstacle that prevents good communication. Jumping to your own conclusions before the speaker has had a chance to finish talking is just as much of a hindrance to the effective communication process as assumptions are. You're not going to be able to accurately receive the message when you've already arrived at your own conclusions even before the speaker has had a chance to finish. Facts become distorted and confused with assumptions when you're busy jumping to conclusions.

A Skewed Focus - Having a focused hat slant too much towards the negative is going to distort your ability to process the messages that you're receiving in an accurate and fair manner. Only focusing on the negative elements, or focusing too much on the flaws is a bad habit that many are guilty of committing, and when your negative perceptions overshadow the rest of the message, effective communication cannot take place when your opinion is already slated towards one point of view no matter what you're being told.

Incongruent Signals - In an exchange of communication, signals and cues are simultaneously being sent just as quickly as they are being received. When there's a lack of consistency between the verbal and non-verbal signals however, that's where the communication tends to slip up and misunderstandings slip into the mix. Effective communicators work hard at making sure their non-verbal cues align with the verbal messages that are being spoken. They avoid saying one thing when their body language is saying something else altogether to avoid confusing their receivers.

Failing to Clarify - Another obstacle that often gets made is failing to clarify the information that you're receiving. This tends to happen a lot when you're pressed for time and in a hurry, and we forget to clarify to make sure we're understanding the speaker the way that they intended to. Both speaker and receiver are guilty of letting this obstacle act as a barrier. The speaker is guilty of this when there's too much unfamiliar jargon, a strong accent, or the use of colloquialisms in the speech, which they might forget to leave out when they assume that the speaker is going to understand just because they understand themselves. As a receiver, we may be guilty of this when we nod, agree, and say yes when the truth is that there may still be several aspects of the message that you're not quite sure you understood well.

The Importance of Practicing Good Communication Skills Everyday

It is possible to achieve the mindful relationships that you want, but you're going to have to work hard at perfecting your communication skills through practice every day. Effective communication can be applied in almost every area of your life, from your work, your family and the relationships that you have with the people in your life. But these skills are not going to develop overnight, and they're certainly not a one-time thing that you practice once and then forget all about.

Great communication skills must be practiced and applied daily, it is the only way you're going to achieve the successful and meaningful interactions that you want. No matter who you may be speaking too. It's a wonderful feeling to be able to connect with people who are so vastly different from you. Everyone around us has a story to tell and a lesson that we all can learn from if we can connect with them well enough to allow them to share their lives with us. As Tibetan-Bhutanese lama, writer and filmmaker, Jamyang Khyentse, so eloquently put it, "*we believe that we are successfully communicating with others, when in fact what's really happening is we're successfully miscommunicating without realizing it*". According to Khyentse, putting a stop to what he referred to as "successful miscommunication" was is, at times, still an arduous process.

If we're being honest with ourselves, most of the time we communicate without being mindful. We're not having mindful discussions when we're not mindful of the words that we use. We're not having mindful discussions is our egos and pride continue to be a factor. We cannot truly connect with another without the genuine desire to do so, and becoming more mindful might just be the missing link that has prevented you from achieving effective communication so far.

Like all the other communication skills, becoming more mindful is also a skill that you can develop with daily practice, discipline and the commitment to do so. To communicate mindfully requires you to develop an awareness of the choices that you make, to be present at the moment, and to be aware of your thought process and the reasons behind your decisions every step of the way. Being able to listen mindfully is especially difficult to achieve if you were still guilty of committing some or all the communication barriers listed above.

Developing the ability to communicate mindfully can be challenging, but it is certainly doable, and it begins with the discipline of practicing the following mindfulness exercises in your everyday life (along with the practice of the other communication skills you have learned throughout this book):

Being Mindful of Your Perceptions - Pause and reflect upon your own perceptions, and give some careful thought to how they were formed. Each time you find yourself forming a perception or assuming, ask yourself on what basis are you forming this opinion. Are they based on concrete facts? Or are they influenced by your own biases and preconceived notions? If your perceptions are not accurate, it might be time to start changing the way that you view things from now on, especially when it comes to the way that you view those who are different from you.

Being Mindful of Others - The communication process involves two people, which means that it is not always all about you. When you focus too much on your own needs, you end up disregarding the opinions and feelings of the other party, which then might lead to misunderstandings and a breakdown in communication when you struggle to relate to them and vice versa. Mindful communication calls for you to develop the ability to focus just as well on the needs of others, the way that you are able to do for yourself. Only when you truly learn to listen to more than just yourself can you start building meaningful relationships that last. Meaningful relationships cannot exist if it is always just about the needs and wants of one person alone without balance.

Being Mindful of Your Internal Chatter - You must learn to quiet the internal chatter within your mind to be able to focus on the conversation at hand.

Stepping away from your own thought process and concerns, and shifting your entire focus towards the speaker enables active listening and mindful communication.

Being Mindful of The Issue at Hand - We can sometimes be guilty of letting our feelings for the speaker stop us from focusing on what the real issue is. If you like the speaker, it is easier to work together and build a meaningful relationship. When you don't like the speaker however, trying to work together and focus on the issue at hand becomes difficult when all you can focus on is your dislike or frustration for the person. Being mindful of your own feelings and learning how to put them aside is how you will learn to work effectively even with those whom you might consider "difficult" or "challenging individuals".

Being Mindful of Boundaries - Boundaries exist for a reason, and that reason is often to maintain a healthy, respectful relationship where both people can feel comfortable interacting with each other without feeling violated or taken advantage of. Being mindful of boundaries is an important factor in your efforts to develop meaningful, lasting relationships. People are more comfortable around you when you demonstrate the ability to remain sensitive and respectful of their needs and what makes them comfortable.

Disconnecting Digitally to Reconnect Once More

As wonderful as technology and social media are, it has also become an obstacle in the communication process. It is incredible to think that the very tool that is supposed to bring us closer than ever (no matter where in the world we may be) is also the very tool that makes us feel more disconnected than we've ever felt before. In fact, technology might even be responsible for some of the anxieties we experience in the communication process.

For example, we have become so accustomed to receiving instant replies that we become paranoid about missing an important text or phone call if we were to step away from our devices for a few minutes. We hardly venture anywhere without our phones these days; it has become permanently attached to us.

Our society has become so reliant on the use of technology to function and communicate that employers are now concerned about how to tailor their communication with the employees who are not permanently attached to their digital devices. It may be hard to fathom, but Pew Research did confirm that at least 11% of Americans are still not using the internet, and this is mostly attributed to several variables, including age, demographics, community, household income, and even educational background. Still, 11% is a small number, which means the other 89% is still heavily reliant on the internet and technology.

There is no doubt that technology has certainly revolutionized the way that we communicate amongst ourselves these days. Conversations over emails and texts have now taken preference over real-time interaction. We can be linked to those who might be across the globe in a matter of minutes and be able to have a virtual conversation with them almost like they were here in front of us. Technology has certainly brought about many changes for the better, but there are some changes in the communication process that aren't exactly for the best. The negative impact technology has left on the communication process might seem minor, but the effects are still nonetheless profound. Here's how technology has had a less than desirable effect on the way we communicate:

It Has Become A Distraction That Is Omnipresent - Technology has now allowed us to stay connected and remain in the virtual space even when we're not in front of the computer. In an emergency, this is a wonderful benefit because you're contactable anytime, anywhere. When trying to have a meaningful conversation, however, it becomes a distraction that makes it hard to stay focused when you're constantly distracted by the notification sounds that come in and the need to respond to a text almost immediately. Technology has made it increasingly difficult to focus on the people in front of you when you're more curious about what's happening on social media. Even when you're having a conversation with someone, your mind could be distracted thinking about what you saw this morning on your newsfeed and wondering what new update has taken place since you last logged into your social media account.

Privacy and Trust Issues Have Become A Greater Concern - It has become so easy for hackers to tap into and gain access to our personal information online that nothing feels safe anymore and everyone becomes a potential suspect. Could this new person sending you a friend request to be a scammer in disguise? Complete and utter privacy online has become nonexistent when it is now so easy for third parties and social media accounts to share and read your personal information and intercept your private data when you sign up for certain services or register for new accounts online. Encryption does offer a sense of security on some level, but it is still impossible to protect every chain of social communication in the online space. Is communicating online, even though text messages and social media, ever completely safe when anyone who is technologically savvy can tap into your private information despite the security precautions you might take?

Communication Lacks the Personal Touch - Staying connections online will never be the same as the bond that is built when you're in the presence of others. The internet has afforded us the benefit of anonymity, allowing us to communicate without having to reveal all the personal details about ourselves. Unfortunately, this also means that building a strong bond of trust is nearly impossible since some people behave differently online than they would if they were interacting in person. Someone could be friendly and chatty online and through texts but becomes socially awkward in a real gathering when they don't have the security of the screen to hide behind.

It Has Led to More Isolation - Ironically, social media has led to an increase in social isolation. The more reliant and comfortable we seem to be with interacting in the social space, the less time we end up spending in the company of others. Amongst the younger generation who grew up relying on technology, social awkwardness is prevalent now more than ever. Social networks have now replaced social connections that we used to form before social media ever existed, and it seems that many have now forgotten how to form bonds with others when they're not done online with a simple like, swipe or use of an emoji. Some people may have a large following on social media, but in reality, they could have little to no real-world friends whom they can count on in their time of need. This lack of support and feeling of isolation then leads to an increase in depression and feeling like you're all alone in the world.

We have become so focused on what's happening in the online world that we miss out on what's happening in real life, with real people. As entertaining as the online world can be, it can never truly replace the comfort, security, and support that can only be felt through the real connections that we make with others. Humans are social creatures, and we always have been. Even before we found the words to communicate and developed the languages that exist today, we still had the desire to reach out and connect with others. The early humans moved in groups and lived in communities, and this was where they thrived best. By working together and being in the company of others. We start relationships, fall in love and get married because we want to feel the love and support of being part of a family. The desire that we have to connect with others and to avoid loneliness has always been a part of who we are, and deep down, that desire has not diminished even with our preference for social media communication.

Technology can never truly replace the happiness that comes with sharing a good laugh with family and friends. It can never replace the warmth of experiencing love, and it will never replace those truly priceless moments that we share when we're in the company of those we love the most. Perhaps it might be time to disconnect digitally to reconnect ourselves with the people who truly matter. Instead of sending a quick text to say hi, pick up the phone or better yet, make plans to meet in person. Anything that you can say over text can be said much better in person. Instead of double-tapping on a picture and laughing by yourself at a funny joke behind the screen, share those moments of laughter instead with in person where there is the opportunity to bond over a shared funny moment or hilarious memory.

Chapter 9: Healing From Negative Energies That Lead To Insomnia, Exhaustiion, And Adrenal Fatigue

Healing: A Substance from Negative Energy

Ideally, this is nothing unexpected to you, yet our bodies are brimming with vitality. Regardless of whether you're comfortable with chi, chakras, emanations, meridians, or some other "life power" vitality; the basic agreement is that this vitality moves through all creatures, so as to keep up well-being and health in mental, physical, passionate, and profound limits.

Similarly, as we have our own vitality, we trade vitality with each other when we take part seeing someone. You've most likely experienced connections (sentimental or not) with "great" vitality; where you are attracted to or pulled in to another for reasons outside of our sensible personality. In a like manner, you've absolutely experienced associations with "awful" vitality; where you feel sincerely depleted collaborating with (or notwithstanding contemplating) the other individual.

Another method for moving toward a troublesome errand or circumstance is to strip it of all passionate charge. Rather than intellectualizing and overthinking the job needing to be done, have a go at utilizing. Remaining centered and disposing of interruptions encourages us to capitalize on our time. Freeing a circumstance of its negative, positive, excruciating, exasperating, irritating, or testing vitality by setting a period farthest point can assist us with staying on track

Vitality seeing someone doesn't simply disseminate in the event that you are physically isolated; this vitality ties us together notwithstanding when separations or conditions set us apart. In a perfect world, the greater part of the vitality we trade and hold in our connections is of the positive, high-vibe nature (or, at any rate, unbiased). Be that as it may, in spite of our earnest attempts to construct important and positive connections, there will consistently be time when life occurs and our connections end up in a condition of disturbance. Indeed, even associations with "great" vitality can wind up in this state. This may happen when we clutch disdain towards a relative, have a dropping out with a companion, separate from a sentimental accomplice, or create strain with a partner. Despite the fact that talking through these distinctions would be the most consistent activity; once in a while, this choice isn't accessible to us as a result of our very own pride (or the pride of the other individual), since regardless we need time to mend, or in some cases for different factors totally out of our control.

At the point when this is the situation, a typical response is to cover the negative feeling. We become repelled from those we were once near, endeavor to divert ourselves with new connections and openings, or will ourselves to disregard a circumstance or individual. While these alternatives enable us to maintain a strategic distance from starting distress, they are not long-haul arrangements as none of them enable us to really manage and discharge the fundamental feeling and vitality. Covering a negative feeling is like covering a weed: regardless of how you spread it up, it will in the long run ascend back to the surface.

Regardless of whether we're mindful of it or not, this adverse vitality not just affects us, keeping us "stuck" inwardly (and at times in different ways), yet — in light of the fact that vitality is a recurrence that ties us to each other — it keeps on influencing the other individual also. For whatever length of time that this vitality is caught, neither one of the persons will have the option to mend completely. Guaranteeing that any caught vitality is discharged and mending can be very incredible, paying little heed to in the event that you would like to restore an association with this individual or not.

All in all, what would we be able to do when we've wound up in a relationship where vitality is "caught"? Here are some particular advances we can take to enable us to discharge this vitality and mend the relationship, even from a far distance:

Know Once more, it is enticing to attempt to "forget about it" when we've had a negative trade or have an uncertain clash with another. Know, in the event that you end up considering (or notwithstanding envisioning about) the individual with which you're vigorous association is crooked; it's a decent sign there is as yet recuperating to do. It's critical to comprehend that caught energies don't need to be completely negative, however, can likewise shape when there is absence of goals in a circumstance.

Comprehend what "mending" signifies. Mending can come in numerous structures. It may be a restored feeling of harmony and tranquillity, it may be the finished gathering of a lost relationship, or it may mean the new and distinctive emphasis of a relationship. Regardless of whether it's accomplished independently or on the whole, recuperating a negative vitality will change a relationship to improve things. This is a significant advance, since when we set out to change or recuperate a relationship, we some of the time look for it to be on our terms. Note that mending the vitality of a relationship could come in numerous structures. Approach this procedure with transparency.

Request help. When you comprehend that recuperating is required and that you have little control of how it occurs; it's an ideal opportunity to request help. This is finished by interfacing with your inward direction framework. While this is usually done through supplication, you can accomplish a comparable discharge through journaling (have a go at composing a letter to an unknown beneficiary requesting help).

Despite your present profound convictions and practice, I urge you to be available to this progression. It doesn't make a difference what or whom you appeal to, simply request help and be available to get it in whatever structure it comes in. During this progression, it is gainful to request help in discharging sentiments like judgment, disdain, fault, and blame. Since you feel advocated in harboring these emotions, it will be hard to understand how you may discharge them. Even more motivation to request help.

As expressed in the last advance, the thought here is to discharge control for how the mending happens. Escape the method for your intelligent personality, which tries to comprehend and design. Escape the method for your personality mind, which looks to be correct. Help is accessible to you from your inward direction framework, which looks to have tranquillity and association. Request it and acknowledge it in whatever structure it might take.

Clear vitality through contemplation. In the event that petition is our medium to request direction and help, reflection is our medium through which we get it. Contemplation is a ground-breaking approach to clear negative vitality and increment positive vitality. I won't continue forever about the constructive outcomes or various types of contemplation. There are a few reflections planned for mending connections over the various controls. I locate this short, guided Releasing Meditation to be an amazing representation device for discharging others, valuing them for what their identity is, and picking bliss for both you and them.

Get a jolt of energy. In case regardless you're feeling off, or just need an additional lift in the vitality division, you can generally work with an expert who assists with vitality mending or clearing. Instances of this are pressure point massage and Reiki. These strategies can be enormously incredible. However, I prescribe you don't depend on them completely, yet keep on doing your own internal work to mend.

Pause. When you are prepared and willing to discharge astounding vitality and mend a relationship, the Universe gets the opportunity to work quick. All things considered, don't anticipate moment satisfaction. You are probably going to encounter a feeling of distress as the reason and vitality of your relationship shifts. Be patient and trust that the Universe is chipping away at your sake, and that you will feel the effect of this move soon.

Concentrating on recuperating remaining vitality from a relationship that appears to have disseminated on the physical plane is a major and significant advance. Clearing old, stale, negative vitality opens space for new, higher-vibe vitality to enter. You'll see that when you set up this training, new connections will show up while former connections will be fixed or advance with new significance.

Recuperating adrenal weakness and turning around the impacts of pressure requires profound, feeding self-care and unwinding... which makes for a fun procedure of revival.

Cortisol—Friend or Worst Nightmare?

Cortisol is your long-haul pressure hormone and a huge supporter of adrenal exhaustion. Generally, our lone long-haul pressure rotated around nourishment being rare. Long haul pressure came as floods, starvations, and wars. During such occasions, we didn't have the foggiest idea where the following dinner was originating from. Today, in the Western world, our long-haul stresses are bound to be monetary pressure, relationship concerns, and vulnerability, or even stresses about our well-being, or the soundness of a friend or family member, yet in addition body weight. For such a significant number of individuals, their first waking contemplations include, "What will I or won't I eat today?" or "How much exercise would I be able to complete today?" and the consistency of these considerations causes customary adrenal pressure.

Vitality seeing someone doesn't simply disperse on the off chance that you are physically isolated; this vitality ties us together notwithstanding when separations or conditions set us apart. In a perfect world, a large portion of the vitality we trade and hold in our connections is of the positive, high-vibe nature (or, at any rate, impartial).

In the event that cortisol tells each cell of your body that nourishment is rare, and your digestion backs off subsequently, and you proceed to eat and practice similarly as you generally have, your garments will gradually get more tightly. With adrenal exhaustion making cortisol advises each cell in your body to store fat, it is troublesome, if certainly feasible, and to diminish muscle to fat ratio until the cortisol issue is settled. We should get to the core of the pressure and either change the circumstance or change the discernment.

Delayed Stress Leads to Adrenal Fatigue

The following biochemical phase of pressure that can happen, particularly if the pressure has been delayed, may include cortisol falling low. On the off chance that you have had a significant level of cortisol yield for some numerous years, your adrenal organs will most likely be unable to stand the pressure, or have the assets to support such nonstop, elevated level cortisol yield and the metabolic results this drives. The adrenal organs were never intended to keep up this example of creation thus cortisol yield plunges. When all is said in done terms, you "wear out." In later occasions, this has turned out to be known as adrenal exhaustion, in light of the fact that the significant indication is a profound and unwavering weakness.

You really feel more terrible after exercise when you are adrenally exhausted, while practice commonly empowers us. Disappointment mounts, since you accept that practicing and eating less are the main answers for weight reduction, yet you can't force yourself to do either in spite of each well-meaning goal. Each time you eat something sweet, you eat excessively, or one more month goes past absent much development. When you consider this, you feel regretful, you may direct mean sentiments toward yourself— and you may quietly lose trust. You presently think, "Who cares?" at whatever point you want to eat something that won't generally sustain you, and the not very good eating proceeds, particularly, an abundance utilization of sugars as you urgently look for vitality. During adrenal fatigue, your garments continue getting more tightly and this equitably adds to your pressure. The endless loop is self-propagating.

As should be obvious, cortisol assumes numerous jobs in our body, and mending adrenal exhaustion side effects to take our cortisol back to ideal levels is fundamental for us to have the option to access muscle to fat ratio to consume it, to feel content, have great vitality, and keep irritation and agony under control.

How Your Nervous System Affects Your Health

At the core of the majority of my methodologies for adrenal exhaustion treatment is the craving for you to rest and to rest well, in a remedial and renewing way. Rest must pursue activity for us to have ideal well-being and amazing fat consuming, and not many individuals nowadays really rest, despite the fact that we may accept we do. A piece of our sensory system called the parasympathetic sensory system (PNS); is dynamic when we really rest. This is the "rest and fix" arm of our sensory system, yet the contrary arm of the sensory system, the thoughtful sensory system (SNS), can rule. For the time being, all you have to know is that on the off chance that you don't get thinner from high-force work out, all things considered, your SNS is prevailing, which is normal with adrenal pressure. On the off chance that you do move weight from this sort of activity, at that point your sensory system is probably going to be all around adjusted.

The Importance of Breathing Well

The other explanation behind this generally concise area about the sensory system here is to make you mindful of the foundation of all my adrenal weariness medications and, similarly as significantly, clarify why I will demand this in the event that you don't remove anything else from this: it has nothing to do with nourishment, and it is completely allowed to everybody. It is breathing, and for a few, it tends to be the way to moving body science from fat stockpiling to fat consuming. How is this conceivable?

The job of the autonomic sensory system (ANS) is to see the inner condition and, in the wake of preparing the data in the focal sensory system (CNS), direct the capacity of your interior condition. The name "autonomic" suggests that it is autonomous of the cognizant personality.

Consider a group of ducks and their infant ducklings. Much the same as ducklings, the autonomic sensory system will consistently pursue the pioneer, and the breath is the main piece of the autonomic sensory system that can be controlled intentionally. Your breath leads. Your body pursues. The manner in which you inhale offers your lone access to your autonomic sensory system, and on the grounds that we inhale 5,000 to 30,000 times each day—or 200 million to 500 million times in your lifetime—it can possibly impact you emphatically or adversely from multiple points of view and truly, this implies you can treat adrenal exhaustion with your relaxing.

Nothing conveys to each cell of your body that you are protected superior to your breath. In the event that you take in a shallow manner, with short, sharp inward breaths and exhalations, at that point you convey to your body that your life is in threat. You have quite recently found out about the course of hormonal occasions that pursues such alert and the job these hormones play in turning fat consuming on or off. How you inhale is likewise a most optimized plan of attack to the manifestations of tension, and conceivably, alarm assaults, paying little mind to what drove you to take in a shallow manner in any case, regardless of whether it was an occasion, a cut-off time, the view of weight and the resulting "need" to surge, or the lifetime propensity for your sensory system. Long, slow breathing that moves your stomach conveys the contrary message to your body—that you are sheltered. Nothing alleviates adrenal weariness and down manages the generation of fat-stockpiling pressure hormones all the more capably.

In this way, arrangement number one is to rehearse diaphragmatic breathing, ensuring your stomach moves in and out as you inhale, rather than your upper chest. To start your adrenal weariness treatment, plan this profound breathing from the outset until it turns into your better approach for breathing (except if you truly need to escape from risk, for example, pummeling your foot on the brake, if another vehicle abruptly drives out before you).

The Importance of Laughter

Another free and amazing asset for treating adrenal exhaustion is giggling. On the off chance that we consider life to be extreme, brimming with diligent work, agony, and drudgery, it will be decisively that.

People can see just their point of view on the planet, as opposed to the world as it genuinely may be. We see the world through channels, yet we don't realize they are there. I am not denying that life can be extreme on occasion or that being straightforward with ourselves on the off chance that we do feel downtrodden about existence is certifiably not something to be thankful for. The adrenal pressure, and our concern, comes when we see the world along these lines and accept that it will never be any extraordinary. For then it won't be.

Consider it. A faith in the perpetual quality of fate is hazardous for each hormonal sign in your body—and as powerhouse of hormones, your adrenal framework is exceptionally influenced. Do your closest to perfect to move your speculation to consider life to be an experience, an adventure and a blessing, loaded with circumstance, a procedure through which we can contribute. An excessive number of individuals are distant from how advantaged their lives are given that the majority of their fundamental needs are met, concerning such a large number of individuals over the globe this is still not the situation. Probably the best, most moving stories I have ever heard have included somebody transforming an awful hardship into their most noteworthy chance. Remember this while dealing with your adrenal fatigue treatment.

Indications of Stress Hormone Production and additionally Adrenal Exhaustion

You feel focused on normally and it feels like you are on red alarm

You put on weight during or after an upsetting period; you may have shed pounds at first during the pressure, yet then recaptured that weight in addition to additional

Body fat has expanded around your center and the back of your arms, and you have developed what I affectionately allude to as a "back verandah"

You want sugar

You cherish espresso and caffeinated drinks—whatever contains caffeine

You alarm (hop) effectively

You don't rest soundly

You frequently wake up inclination unrefreshed

You in some cases wake up feeling like you've been hit by a transport

You feel good on the off chance that you can rest until 8 or 9 a.m., as opposed to emerging somewhere in the range of 5 and 7 a.m.

If you don't rest by 10 p.m., you get a revitalizing burst of energy and wind up remaining wakeful until at any rate 1 a.m.

You routinely feel tired yet wired

You hold liquid

Your face looks "puffy" or swollen now and again (and different causes have been precluded)

You are a worrier; you don't unwind effectively

You are a "control crack"

Your body feels substantial and pain-filled on occasion, despite the fact that you don't have an ailment that warrants this

Your circulatory strain is high

Your circulatory strain is low, or at the low finish of ordinary

You get mixed up effectively, however, especially when you go from sitting to standing rapidly

You feel on edge effectively

You will in general experience low mind-sets with no known other reason

Your breathing will in general be shallow and very quick

148

You experience "air craving" (and different causes have been discounted)
You battle to state "No"
You snicker short of what you used to
You feel like everything is pressing

Stress Hormones Solutions

Similarly, as significant, if not the most significant part of avoiding adrenal weakness for a reasonable and proper pressure hormone reaction, is the utilization of the passionate well-being methodologies just as cognizant relaxing. I know breathing sounds too easy to even think about treating adrenal pressure yet diaphragmatic breathing (making your stomach move in and out as you inhale, rather than your upper chest) can actually completely change you. Furthermore, I don't state that delicately.

Practice therapeutic yoga, Pilates, judo, or qigong at least two times every week for about a month. Build up a day by day practice for exceptional outcomes. My most loved is a training known as Stillness

Through Movement. Focus on a breath-centered practice.

Spend five minutes every day concentrating on and offering voice to every one of an amazing part for which you are appreciative; you can't be focused when you feel thankful.

With the direction of a botanist, take some adrenal weariness supplement herbs. Not all home-grown medication is made equivalent, be that as it may, so you need to guarantee the brand you take is legitimate. Watch that it has been tried by an elevated level quality-control framework and that the dynamic fixings said to be in the item are in fact present, just as no contaminants. Natural medication can be taken in a fluid tincture structure or as tablets. Most of the accompanying adrenal depletion herbs are adaptogens, meaning they help the body adjust to worry by tweaking the pressure reaction.

They include:

Withania (Ashwagandha) for the worriers

Rhodiola for the show rulers or sometimes for the worriers

Siberian ginseng (eleuthero) for the exhausted ladylike

Panax ginseng for the completely exhausted (transient utilize as it were)

Licorice, particularly if your circulatory strain is on the low finish of ordinary

Dandelion leaves, particularly in the event that you hold liquid

The adrenals additionally love nutrients B and C, and to battle adrenal weariness I more often than not enhance both: the Bs as a multivitamin or a straight B-complex , in addition to 4–5g every day of nutrient C , ideally in powdered structure with included calcium and magnesium, with the portions split throughout the day. On the off chance that you are on an oral prophylactic pill, stick to 2g of nutrient C every day.

The Restorative Power of Good Food

In spite of the fact that I regularly prescribe enhancements of herbs as well as supplements for adrenal exhaustion, keep in mind the recuperating and therapeutic intensity of nourishment the manner in which it comes in nature. Taking enhancements isn't motivation to eat a low quality, low-supplement diet. I just prescribe supplements where suitable and particularly to aid battle against adrenal weariness and the reclamation of well-being. There is no pill that can compensate for a lousy method for eating.

Chapter 10: Developing Your Empathic

Gift

On looking at the pros and cons of being an empath, one thing is evident. Focusing on the positives of being an empath coupled with learning how to maintain and further develop your gift will change your outlook on life! Instead of having to live cautiously through each day, avoiding certain places and people, there are specific steps that you can take to ensure that you are shielded from negative energies and only take in positive vibes. These steps will help you grow emotionally and mentally.

Here are a few ways for you to ensure you maintain your emotional stability and overall your sanity:

Meditation to Quiet Your Body and Mind - With all the thoughts, emotions and energies cruising through you, finding ways to maintain your mental peace is a necessity. You cannot talk about internal peace without mentioning meditation. Meditation exercises are the perfect way to calm yourself down, especially when in turmoil! There are various types of meditation; therefore you might need to research to know what works best for you. You can also download guided meditations to help with breathing exercises and help your body to relax, centering all your energies. A 10-15 minute session daily should be sufficient.

Find Ways to Release your Energy – Since you take in other people's energies, it is imperative that you find ways to balance out or get rid of your negative vibes. One way can be through journaling where you put all your thoughts and frustrations into words. Another way would be to pick a physical activity like a sport or going to the gym. Something that you love that will help in centering your energies and helping your balance out your emotions.

Learn to Say "NO" - This is one of the biggest complications for empaths. The constant need to make everyone happy makes it difficult to say 'NO'. You must always remember that saying no to others is saying yes to yourself as this is the only way you will be able to maintain a healthy level of emotional and mental stability. Being an empath does not mean that you always have to go above and beyond for the needs of others.

Make Balance An Art - You have to manage your gift while ensuring a great balance between your emotional and spiritual sides. As a healer, learn to heal yourself as you specialize in healing others. Also remember to balance out your human ego as your skill develops and grows!

Find your Own Support System - As an empath, you are automatically cast into the role of helper and emotional counselor for everyone around you. Taking in that many emotions and energies without having your own support system can leave you washed out and worn out. Therefore, it is important that you have a friend or two who you can call on whenever you feel overwhelmed. This should be someone that knows you well, and if you are lucky enough, a fellow empath who can understand and relate to the challenges you are facing.

Learning Shielding Techniques for Empaths - In most cases, you will have almost no control over the energies you absorb. In worst case scenarios where you are surrounded by energy vampires, it is paramount that you learn how to protect yourself from negative emotions and energies. As discussed in chapter two, this will need you to create some energy boundaries beyond which negative energy cannot penetrate.

Learn How To Develop Your Gift By Reading Widely - All the information on energies, healing, and centering techniques are all available online through different books and blogs. You just need to learn how to improve your ability to read energies (psychometry), how to develop your psychic abilities (clairvoyance), among other abilities.

Connect to Nature - Empaths have a special connection to animals and nature. Use this ability to feel their energies to calm yourself. Take long walks in nature to calm down. You can also take the time to sit with your pet and just feel their energy.

Learn to Control your Emotions - Empaths get major highs and lows when it comes to emotions. This is because they are affected by emotions of the people around them. For newbie empaths, this can cause major emotional instability in terms of mood swings. Controlling this requires you to learn how to reduce your impulsive nature. Taking time to relax using breathing techniques can help you stabilize your emotions prior to taking any action.

Coping Mechanisms - Empaths are able to know when someone isn't being truthful. One of the ways to maintain your gift is to learn coping mechanisms for such situations. What do you do when you can clearly see your loved one is lying through their teeth? In order to cope, you must know how to use your ability to reach out to people, to calmly confront them and get the truth from them. This might be difficult at first considering that you are highly sensitive, but with enough patience and practice, you will be good to go in no time.

Points to Ponder About Empaths
If you are an empath, you need to realize that you were born that way and it is not something to despise. Others may see it as a disadvantage but do not you're your life that way. Just because other people don't understand what being an empath is

about doesn't mean you are the problem. Being an empath is a gift with its own numerous benefits. Therefore, when properly focused, this gift can become of importance and benefit to you and the people around you.

In conclusion, there some major takeaway points from the book that you need o focus on in order to appreciate empaths and their gifts:

●Empaths are affected by energies in their environment, whether it is from people, animals or even plants. These energies could also be positive or negative.

●Empaths are highly sensitive to emotional stimuli which when not controlled can lead to emotional instability and mood swings.

●Empaths are the most affected by energy vampires. Energy vampires are people who suck your energies, giving you negative energy and emotions.

●To counter negative emotions, you ought to cut off energy vampires from your life or find a way of shielding yourself from their negative emotions and energies. (Emotional shielding).

●Being an empath comes with its own set of major challenges. An empath cannot control the kinds of energies they absorb while in public areas. Negative energies can, in turn, affect an empath's physical, mental and emotional health.

●To develop as an empath, it is necessary that one learns how to be calm through techniques like meditation. Learn to develop yourself in terms of building the gift. Finally, strive to find a balance in your energy and emotions by getting a support system.

In conclusion, being an empath can be a blessing or a curse depending on how you choose to perceive it. This means that how you choose to use the gift is all up to you. Therefore, strive to develop it to become the blessing it was intended to be!

Chapter 11: Crystals And Gemstones For

Empaths

Empaths are gifted individuals who are naturally magnetic. They are intuitive healers—empaths tend to feel emotions deeply. They also have the ability to absorb negative emotions that are not theirs. They take on other people's emotional burdens. This can be overwhelming and dangerous at the same time and could lead to various physical symptoms such as fatigue, headaches, flu, colds, back pains, and even fever. In addition, it could result in panic disorders, social anxiety disorder, and depression.

This is the reason why empaths use crystals to clear their energy and emotions. The following are protective and healing stones to keep your aura strong and ward off negative energies and entities:

Hematite

This is a grounding stone that keeps your aura connected with the world. This semi-precious stone helps you focus and stay in control of your emotions and energy. It brings you inner peace and it helps transforms negative energy to love. This stone also balances the root chakra.

Actinolite

This stone shields you from negative energy. It helps improve your sense of self-worth and inner strength. It also heals your aura and fixes the gaps that can result from sickness, external negativity, and psychic attack. Furthermore, this stone helps you connect with your spirit guides.

Amethyst

This crystal helps detoxify the body and helps treat different types of mental health issues such as depression and chronic stress. It also helps promote temperance and treats addiction to food, alcohol, and sex. This crystal has strong protective properties and can help enhance psychic abilities. It repels negative vibrations so it can be extremely beneficial to empaths.

Aquamarine

Aquamarine has strong shielding properties. It releases fear and anxiety. It is also beneficial for those who are suffering from depression and grief. This stone has strong metaphysical and healing properties.

Aragonite

This stone is usually found in Spain, Namibia, and Mexico. It has a strong grounding and calming properties. It also helps increase one's self-worth and self-confidence.

Azurite

This stone strengthens the energy in different chakras. It improves creativity and helps relieve stress. It also stimulates psychic gifts such as intuition and clairvoyance. This stone calms your emotions and it improves the health of your spine.

Barite

This stone balances the energy by improving the flow of energy in your body, breaking up energy blockages. Barite can enhance dream recall. It can also help you solve old problems and detoxify your body.

Amber

This stone is a potent protection from depression and stress. It helps you absorb more positive energy and improves the overall level of your happiness. It also promotes self-healing and it has the ability to transform negative energy into positive energy.

Amazonite

If you exhibit self-damaging behavior, this is the perfect stone for you. This stone helps increase one's self-worth and helps to strengthen your physical body. It also improves the function of your heart and balances your energy centers.

Blue Lace Agate

This stone brings happiness and peace. It also helps reduce family conflict and alleviate muscular tension and stress.

Dragon Vein Agate

This stone balances your energetic field. It helps reduce the negative emotions and assists you in finding your life purpose.

Fire Agate

This stone is hard to find and it has strong grounding properties. You can wear this gemstone as a protective shield against potential harm and negative energy.

Kunzite

This stone is great for people who are dealing with addiction. It helps reduce stress, moodiness, and depression. It also improves self-esteem and has a calming effect.

Lepidolite

This awesome stone can help treat various mental health issues such as depression, anxiety, stress, and substance abuse. It helps cure compulsive behavior and it is great for those who are experiencing emotional stress, grief, or trauma.

Lapis Lazuli

This is an energy cleanser that helps eliminate negative emotions from your system. It also helps you tap your psychic abilities and connect with your spirit guides. It has strong protective qualities.

Malachite

This semi-precious stone has strong healing properties. It cleans your auric fields and helps reduce depression and tension.

Moldavite

This stone is best for empaths that act as spiritual healers. It has strong grounding and self-healing properties.

Mangano Calcite

This stone heals your inner child and promotes self-love. It also relieves tension and anxiety. It gives you the courage and strength to deal with trauma and emotional pain as well.

Lodestone

This stone can eliminate negative emotions such as fear, anger, grief, and unhealthy attachments. It also helps remove toxic blocks from your body.

Blue Spinel

This stone gives you a strong sense of hope, so it is a potent protection from depression. It also aligns your physical and spiritual bodies.

Sunstone

Sunstone has powerful grounding and protective elements. Aside from increasing libido and sexual energy, it is also a potent stress reliever.

Sugilite

This stone clears emotional blocks and it can help you cope with various challenges in life.

Thulite

Thulite helps you tap into your psychic powers and helps treat pain and diseases caused by emotional neglect.

Tiger's Eye

This is a powerful stone that helps improve your intuition. It also helps manifest your thoughts, dreams, and plans into your physical reality.

Blue Topaz

This stone brings peace into your life. It protects you from external negative emotions and stress. It also brings success and good fortune.

Peridot

This stone helps heal heartaches and in balancing your relationships. It can be useful in treating anxiety, depression, and intense anger. It also acts as a natural protective shield for empaths.

Pyrite

This is one of the most grounding stones. It can protect you from energy vampires and improve your outlook on life.

Prehnite

This stone is powerful because it helps you find your spiritual path. It also has strong protective properties.

Celestial Quartz

This stone helps repair the brain cells that were damaged due to alcohol and drug abuse. This stone can also protect you from psychic attacks.

Moonstone

This stone helps relieve stress and anxiety. It improves your decision-making skills, as well as promotes reconciliation.

Onyx

This is a powerful stone that absorbs emotional abuse and negativity. It also promotes optimism and helps remove excessive attachment to people and things.

Obsidian

This stone is extremely useful for empaths and people with strong psychic abilities. It helps reduce stress and absorbs negative energy. However, take note that you should not wear this as jewelry.

Opal

This popular gemstone increases your self-worth and self-esteem. It also strengthens your intuition.

White Pearl

Pearl balances your emotions and improves emotional stress. It also has a calming effect.

Bloodstone

This helps reduce stress and remove emotional blockages.

Boji Stones

This stone aligns the chakras and balances the energy field of the body.

Blue Calcite

This stone is soothing and helps remove the tension and stress from your body.

Bronzite

Bronzite empowers you to take care of yourself. It also helps you achieve clarity and certainty.

Turquoise

This stone cleanses, aligns, and strengthens your energy fields and chakras. It protects you from psychic attacks and has strong healing properties. If you're going through heartbreak, this is the perfect stone for you.

Black Tourmaline

A calming stone, black tourmaline helps dispel fear and negativity. It helps heal mental disorders and also dissolves negative energy.

Unakite

This stone promotes optimism. It helps improve one's self-esteem and can be useful for people who are going through divorce or separation.

Variscite

This helps ease fear, depression, and emotional pain. It increases self-confidence and promotes emotional stability.

Rubellite

This stone balances your energy and helps ease emotional pains. It also balances your electrochemistry.

Rose Quartz

Like rubellite, rose quartz helps heal emotional pain and bring peacefulness and joy. It has strong anti-aging properties and aligns your mental, emotional, and astral bodies. It increases creativity and self-confidence as well.

Smoky Quartz

This stone eases feelings of panic, fear, and depression. It also clears negative energy and is a great mood elevator. It stimulates the Kundalini energy and increases creativity.

Snow Quartz

This stone can protect you from negative vibrations and can help strengthen your intuition and psychic abilities.

Citrine

This is one of the most popular stones. It helps treat self-destructive patterns and increases self-esteem. It also promotes hope, optimism, and cheerfulness.

Coral

This beautiful stone helps improve your emotional health. It also has strong protective qualities.

Emerald

Emerald helps develop your clairvoyant abilities and helps treat depression.

Fluorite

This helps remove drama from your life and helps you maintain healthy personal boundaries.

Dioptase

This stone improves your overall well-being. It also has strong healing properties.

Sapphire

This stone helps strengthen your psychic abilities. It also helps you connect with your spirit guides.

Rhodonite

This stone provides emotional support. It soothes stress, anxiety, and heartache. It also reinforces the power of affirmation and chanting.

Ruby

This stone gives you courage, energy, and confidence. It helps you cope with life's daily pressures and improve your self-esteem.

Sodalite

This stone is usually used during meditation. It is so powerful that it helps heal emotional issues. It is perfect for empaths as it helps reduce oversensitivity. A potent treatment for panic attacks, sodalite calms the mind and helps you see psychic visions.

Blue Jade

This stone helps you overcome external challenges and difficult situations.

Jade

This stone is believed to bring good luck and peace and helps remove negativity from your life. It helps you remain calm and grounded even when faced with difficulties.

Hematite

This is a centering and grounding stone that increases your resistance to stress.

Red Jasper

This stone serves as a protective shield from negativity.

Dragon's Blood Jasper

If you're surrounded with toxic people, this is the perfect stone for you. This stone helps ward off negativity and psychic attacks.

Jet

Jet helps cure depression and also promotes optimism.

Clear Calcite

This amazing stone helps clear your aura. It also balances your chakras.

Emerald Green Calcite

This stone helps remove energy blocks and helps you let go of issues that may prevent you from finding true love. It also improves your intuition.

Orange Calcite

This stone increases your inner strength and clears your body and mind.

Violet Calcite

Violet calcite can help you deal with grief. It also helps eliminate intense emotions and negative thoughts.

Carnelian

Aside from increasing optimism, carnelian has grounding and healing properties.

Red Calcite

Red calcite brings stability. It also increases emotional strength and helps detoxify your body.

Blue Chaldony

Blue chaldony helps calms your nerves and it helps overcome anxiety.

Chrysocolla
This stone helps in cleansing your auric field, alleviating negative feelings such as guilt and fear.
Green Aventurine
This amazing stone is not only attractive, but it also has strong protective properties. It helps eliminate your fear and anxiety. It also helps improve mind and body connection.

Crystals and gemstones are not only decorative. They can also act as a shield. So, if you want to ward off unwanted negativity and emotions, you should consider using the crystals and gemstones mentioned in this list.

Chapter 12: Overcoming The "Energy Vampire"

What Is An Energy Vampire?

In ancient lore, Vampires were known as creatures of the darkness that fed off the blood of their victims by sucking the life out of them...In the same way, an energy vampire is a person, place, or thing that drains you of your own precious energy. Remember back to the beginning of the book when I talked about how everything in the universe is essentially energy? Well, Energy vampires are forms of energy that feed off the life energy of others. Kind of like a leech, or in spookierterms... a vampire!

Common day energy vampires are usually people that can only survive by means of breaking down others and taking their energy. However, they can arise in many different shapes and forms. Being an Empath, it is essential to realize how severe this can effect your life due to your sensitivity. You are like an unguarded; juicy peace of meat in the eyes of an energy vampire, and I assure you, they'll want a bite!

How Can I protect My Sacred Energy?

There are a many ways to protect your energy. The most powerful technique that I advise you to learn is simply to shine bright! Remember, energy vampires thrive in the darkness and can only effect you if you allow them to. You being an Empath, are naturally a radiant being. All you must do is allow your light to shine through the illusion and illuminate the darkness. Not only will this scare off any energy vampires instantly, it will also help you embrace your nature fully, and live a more vibrant, impactful life.

You will become the beacon of light where people from all over will be attracted to you. This will ultimately help you on your journey and you will become a teacher to those who have lost their way. However, this is a process and may take a bit of time. This can only be of use to you until you are strong enough to recognize your power, and claim that shit for the taking!

OK...What Are The Other Ways?

Shining bright is my personal favorite and I find it the most beneficial. But I understand that for an untrained Empath, this can be a challenging task.Below I've provided a list of simple, yet powerful ways to say"No"to energy vampires and claim your energy for the taking.

Surround yourself with people that build you up, not break you down. Empaths are known to absorb other people's energy. If you are hanging around a lot of negative energy that does not serve you, you will begin to become more like this energy or have a meltdown. Learn to distance yourself form these people and find others that bring out the light in you.

Change the environment you place yourself in. Often times Empaths are overwhelmed with all of the commotion around them. If you are surrounding yourself with chaotic environments like large crowds of people and stressful situations. Chances are, you will embody that stress and commotion around you and internalize it. Instead, practice venturing out into **nature** or taking a walk in the park. Begin to feel out the environments that you are exposed to and start heading in the direction of the one that makes you feel most at peace.

Learn to say"NO", even though your used to saying"YES". Often times we lend out our energy to people and circumstances that do not return the favor. Have you ever spent so much energy and time into something for someone else only to realize that they aren't giving you anything in return? This is a huge signal that they are an energy vampire. Empaths are excellent givers because helping people is our natural state. However, many times the things we choose to serve are actually leaching our energy from us **with**our consent. If you don't want to do something, you don't have to, that simple. If you feel like your being pressured into

180

something that you'renot comfortable with, begin to firmly say"No"and then kindly walk away. The choice is yours, choose wisely whom to lend your energy to.

Create a small group or community that supports you. It is vital to get your energy flowing and active in a healthy way. Each and every person has their own energy field that surrounds them. Begin to experiment with friends and family that are beneficial to your personal energy field as well as theirs. It is Crucial to surround yourself with energy that resonates with you, and promotes your health and happiness. The more you surround yourself with positive energy, the more positivity you will absorb and your life will begin to change for the best.

Empaths are highly sensitive energy sponges. Do yourself a favor and distance yourself from the negativity in your life to bring out more positivity.

How Do I Attract Positivity?

We live in a law of attraction based universe. Like attracts like. Dark attracts dark. Light attracts light. And so on…To begin to attract more positive energy into your life, you must first flush out as much negativity within and without as possible. If you can't seem to do this immediately do not worry. Slowly and surely change your habits and move further away from things that no longer serve you.

What If I Find Myself Alone?

If you are primarily living in a negative environment, you will most likely find yourself alone at some point on your journey towards a positive life. If this is you out there, start to embrace the alone time that you get. **The best relationship you can have, is the relationship you have with yourself.** Keep pressing on and create as much of whatever you desire to attract within yourself. Eventually, the universe will see you radiating positivity and give you more positive things. You will then accumulate more and more of that energy, and energy vampires will begin to lose their power over you or vanish completely.

 And then you'll just say... "Feels So Good To Be Alive Baby"!!!

Chapter 13: Managing Criticisms

Being an HSP you are more sensitive to criticisms, you are likely to take them personally. These are the things you can do to lessen the pain and benefit from negative feedback.

Refuse to be labeled

Accepting a label somebody has given you lets the other person dictate who you are. You are who you are no matter what people say.

If you're at fault, acknowledge it and apologize appropriately

If somebody says that you're late again and you really are, say, "Yes, I'm late, I'm sorry." This will let the other person know that you recognize your mistake and that you care about how they made them feel.

Ask for clarification

Criticism can be vague, which makes it hard to be used constructively. If you don't understand what the critic is saying, request that he/she be more specific. For example, you are told that you are being lazy. You can ask, "What makes you say that I'm lazy?" or "What should I work harder on?"

You may not control your feelings of getting but if somebody says something bad about you, the chapter on managing emotions will help you lessen the effect of negative emotion and recover fast.

Giving Complaints

Since you are an HSP and an Empath, you will be quite hesitant to say something that might offend another person. If you need to give a complaint, these steps will make it easier:

Name the problem

Say exactly what your problem is. Be specific, brief, and clear. Stick to the facts and avoid assuming things.

State your feelings

Say what you feel and what you think of the problem, as it is. Don't exaggerate. Don't even try to shame the other person, maintain the focus on yourself. Say, "I feel uncomfortable because of loud music", instead of, "You should be ashamed that you don't care about what others feel about your music."

Specify what you want

Say what you want directly. Don't beat around the bush, because you'll just become more frustrated when the other person doesn't get them. Avoid talking in riddles, thinking that the other person can interpret them.

Ask for reasonable changes one at a time so that others can manage to do it.

Remember that your mind tends to magnify emotions, so what you think will be devastating to others may not really matter to them at all. Try not to worry about others' feelings too much.

By now, you may have realized that there are a lot of things you can do to make life easier for you. But wait; what about handling emotions? Don't worry; there is a chapter for that.

Chapter 14: The Art Of Persuasion

Basics of persuasion
Persuasion is making people follow your idea or support you in doing something. This happens in arranged interactions such as business meetings, job interviews, and in daily social interactions. For persuasion to be effective the individual that is using this method must know some basics.

The topic of persuasion is very important as it determines the effort and tactics used in persuasion. If the topic is too complex for the audience, it might not be easy to convince them and therefore all the efforts available that seem effective can be employed to convince the audience. The topic might also be too complex for you as the persuader, and therefore, seeking help from the experts is always useful. It might not sound good when you give wrong information about something and expect people to believe you.

The age and level of education of the people you are talking to is also an important aspect to have in mind. This helps to choose the language and approach to use to persuade them; the method you use to persuade children is not the same as the one used to persuade adults or students in college. Also, experts in health cannot be persuaded using the same language as that used to persuade mothers who have little knowledge in the field of health.

Tools for persuasion which include facts and aids such as videos should be considered and their accessibility; you cannot use something you do not have, and therefore as you prepare for the persuasion always keep this in mind.

Methods of Persuasion
Reciprocation

The society operates on the principle that I give you back what you gave me. This can be in the form of behavior, favor or even something physical. For example, if I helped you when you needed help, when I need help you will help me as well. This is because, after I help you, you become obligated to do help me at a later time when I need it and not to the other person who did not help you. This method of persuasion works because the groups in the society that uses the principle of reciprocation are always competitive compared to the groups that do not use. Members of such a group will gladly give out resources because they know that it is a credit that will be paid back when the time comes. Therefore, when you are persuading people, master the skill of sharing or exchanging favors with the ones you intend to persuade and you will create a partnership that would enable you to get what you want from them.

Use of Scarcity

According to research the merit of something does not matter unless it is put in a context where it is required. Simply put, people will always be in need of what they cannot get at that time. When you have an idea, and what you are offering to the people is something that they can easily get it somewhere else, there is a likelihood that they will not listen to it and take it. Therefore, for a persuade to be effective in using this method, he or she should present arguments that have many advantages to make the other party realize that your idea is the one with more merits and move in your direction. Again, it is important to know that sometimes people are interested in what they would lose, because in some instance what one loses can be more valuable than what he or she is gaining. Therefore, it is also important to always good to explain on the losing side to persuade those who feel that they will lose the most important thing or part. However, to make sure that the negative side does not affect your persuasion, bring in new information to guide them to your side. There are people, who are quick to analyze situations, and it is not easy to convince them, always do your research well to make sure that they are not left out.

The Use of Authority

Most people trust information from the expert or from powerful people; if it is from the experts then it is true. This one becomes difficult because it is not always that a doctor will talk to people about health issues or a lawyer about legal matters, but you can always include them in your conversation to assure the people that what you are telling them is the knowledge that is approved by experts. If this is not possible you can use terminologies from the field of your topic and quote phrases or words spoken by experts in the field to establish the authority of your information.

Use of the Consistency

Persuasion is sometimes a process, and you must involve the people in the process up to a point that they feel that there is no way back. This is done during a discussion when decisions are made at each stage and there is no reversal of a decision that is made in the previous stage. The persuader can use a language such as, we can now count on you, right? The person agrees to the statement, and the next state is welcomed for discussion. The fact that they agreed in the previous stage prompts them to agree to what they are being asked regardless of what they feel about at that stage.

Use of Liking

People will always agree to follow the people they have a liking for, and dismiss the other person. Persuaders have known this behavior and mostly use it to their advantage. That is why most advertisements are done by famous and most like celebrities; the advertiser knows that if they like the person, they would tend to like the product that is associated with that personality. The thinking of the audience is that by using the product, you are part of the person advertising the product. The same idea can be used to support big ideas and programs.

9 781989 920497